Cats On the Water

Coloring book

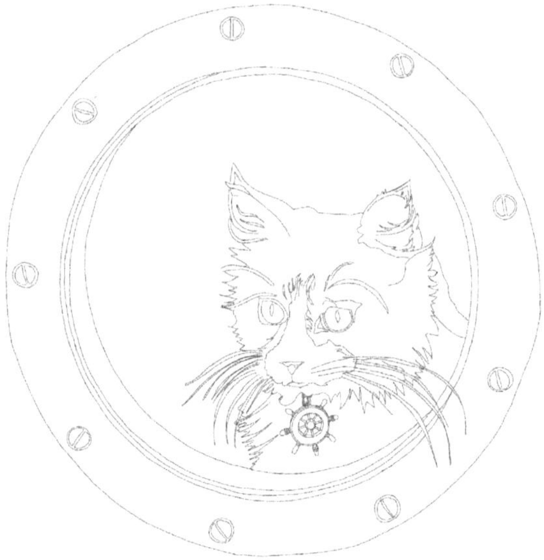

By Marina Zale

This Book Belongs To

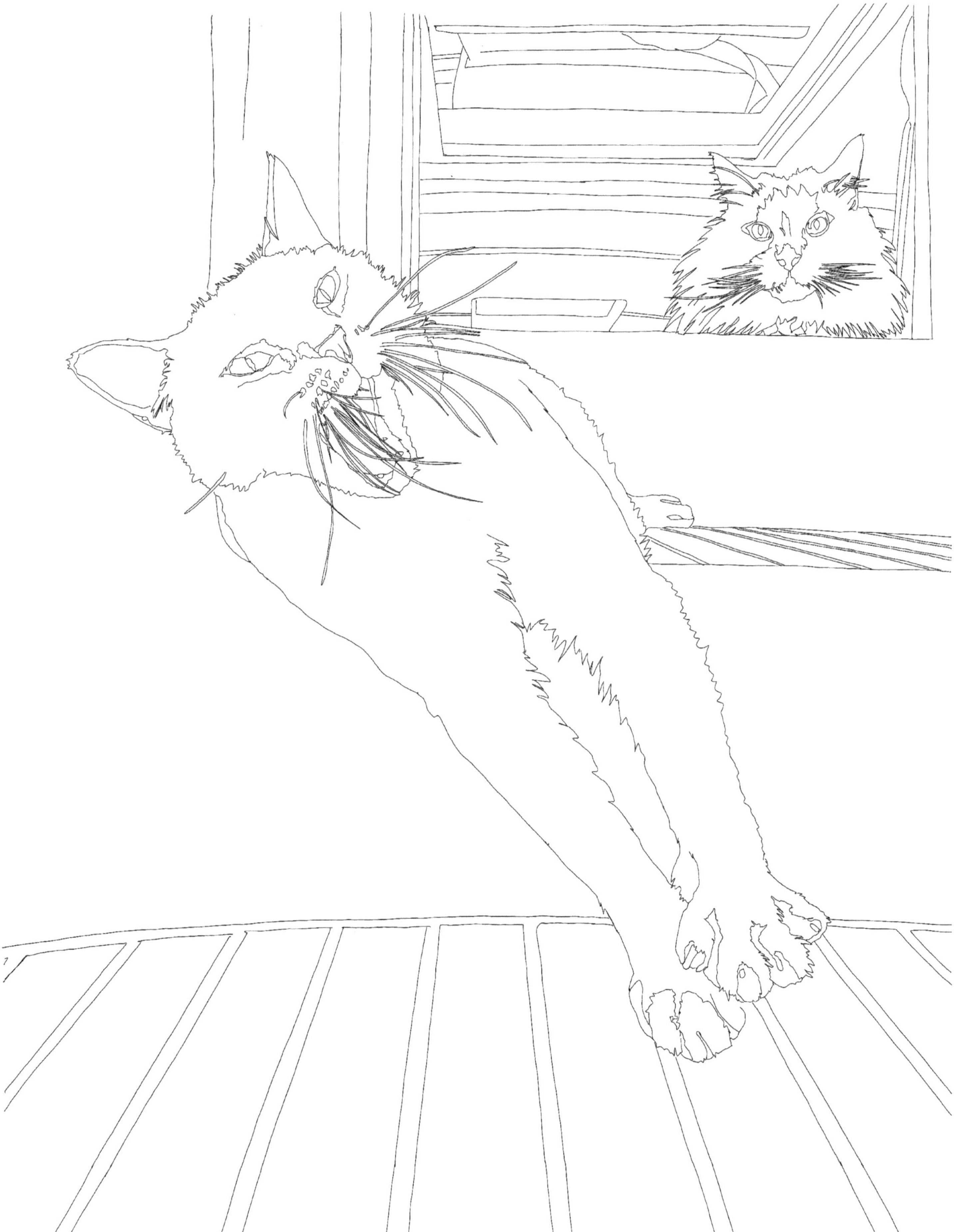

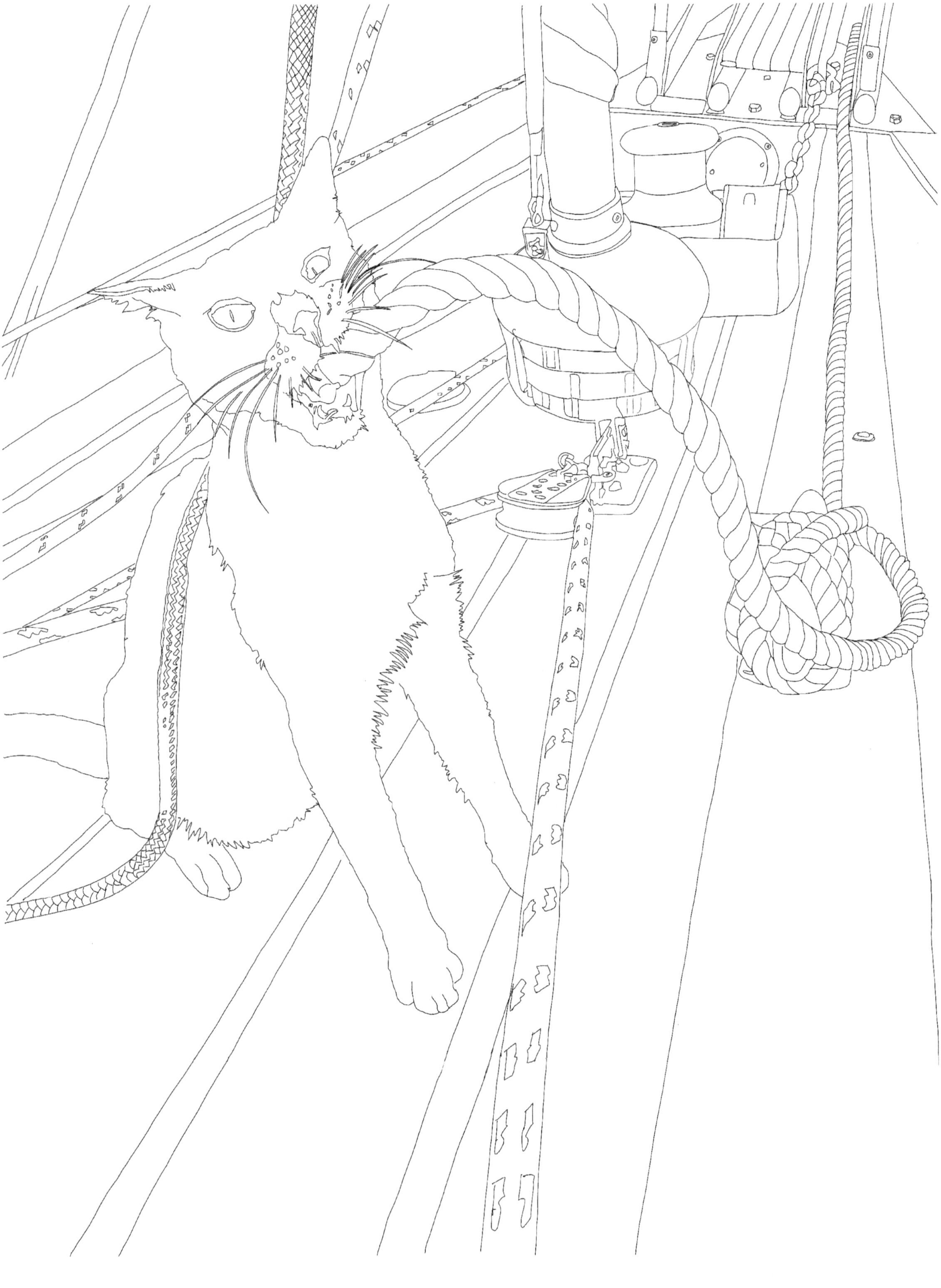

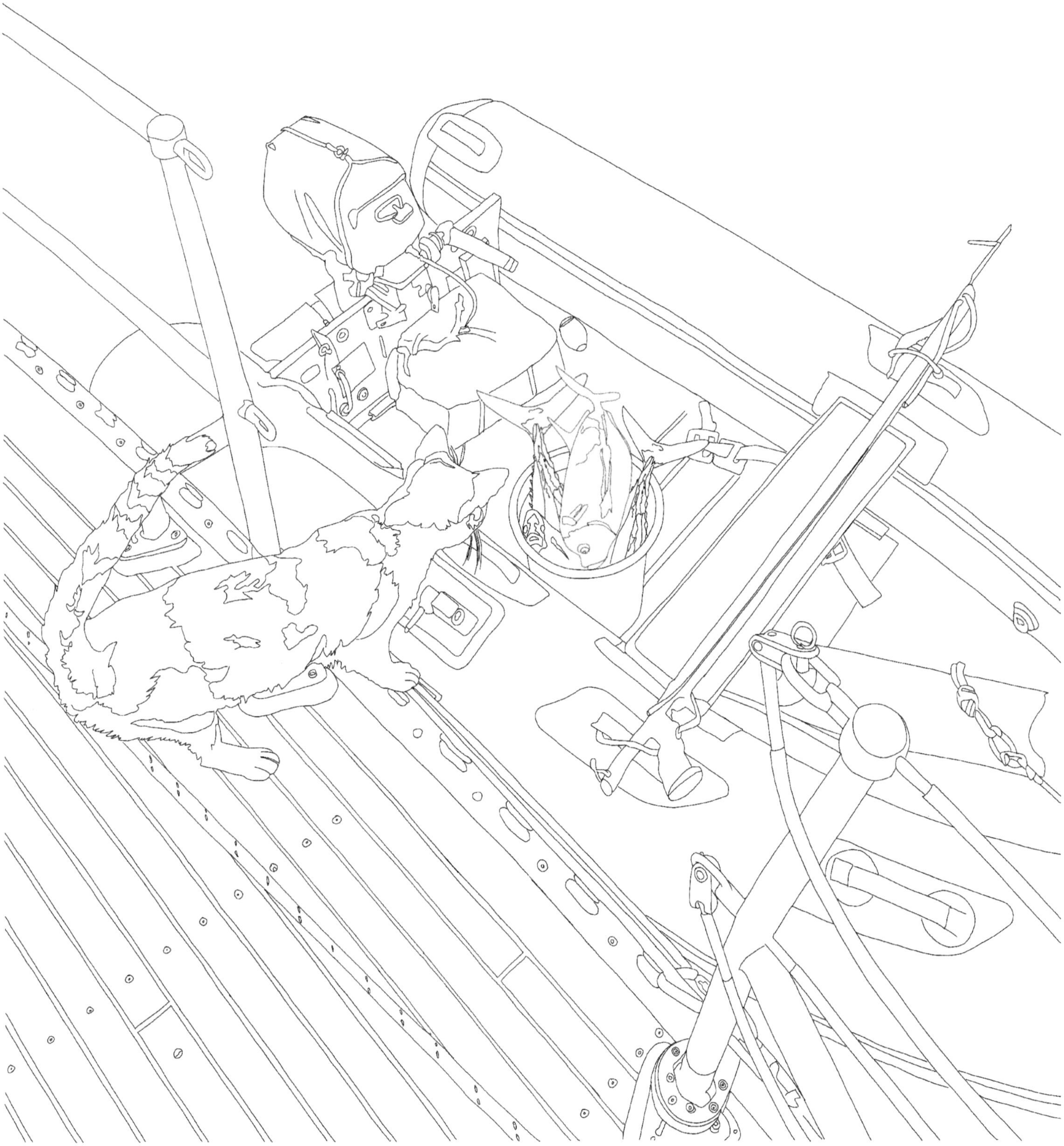

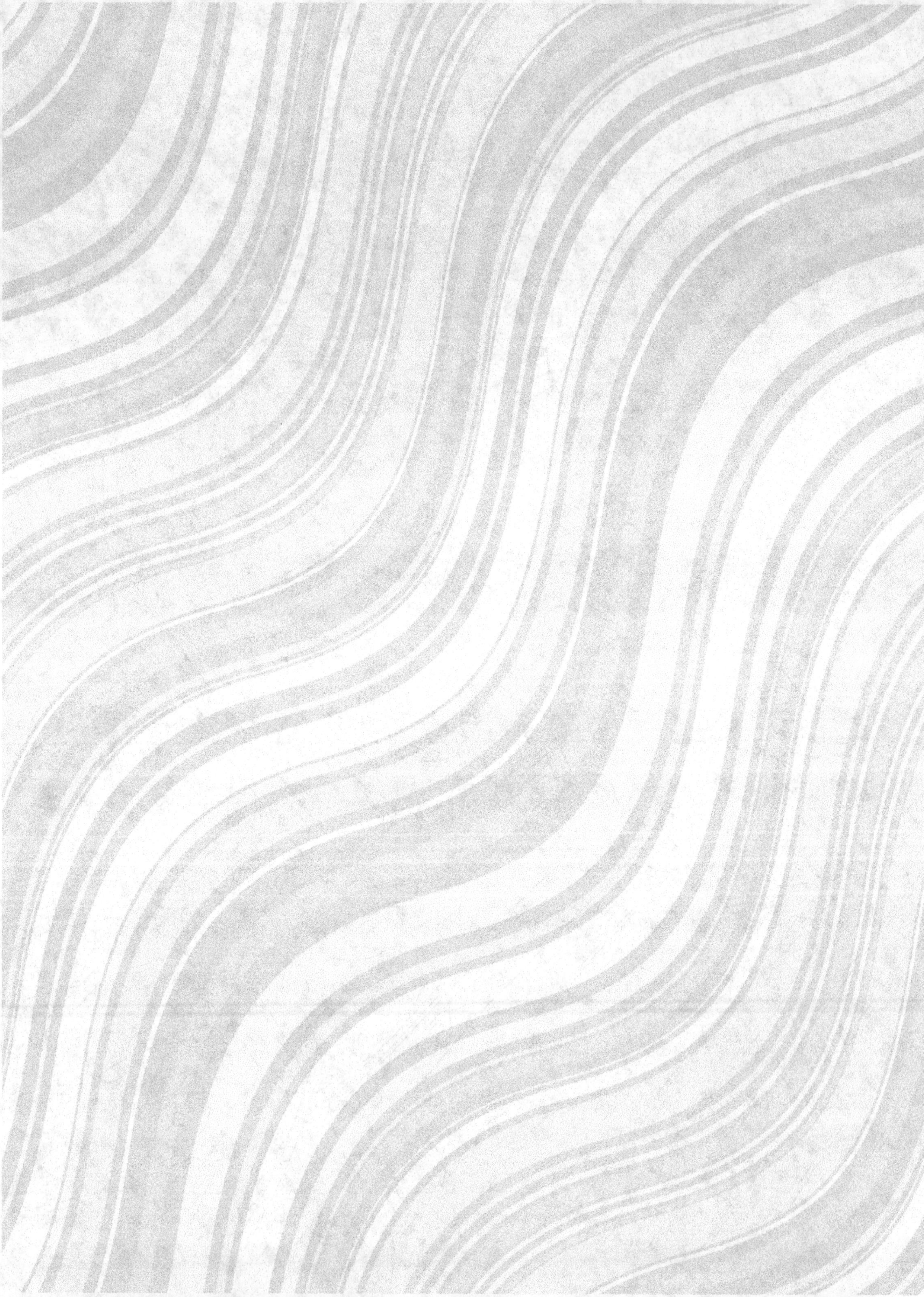

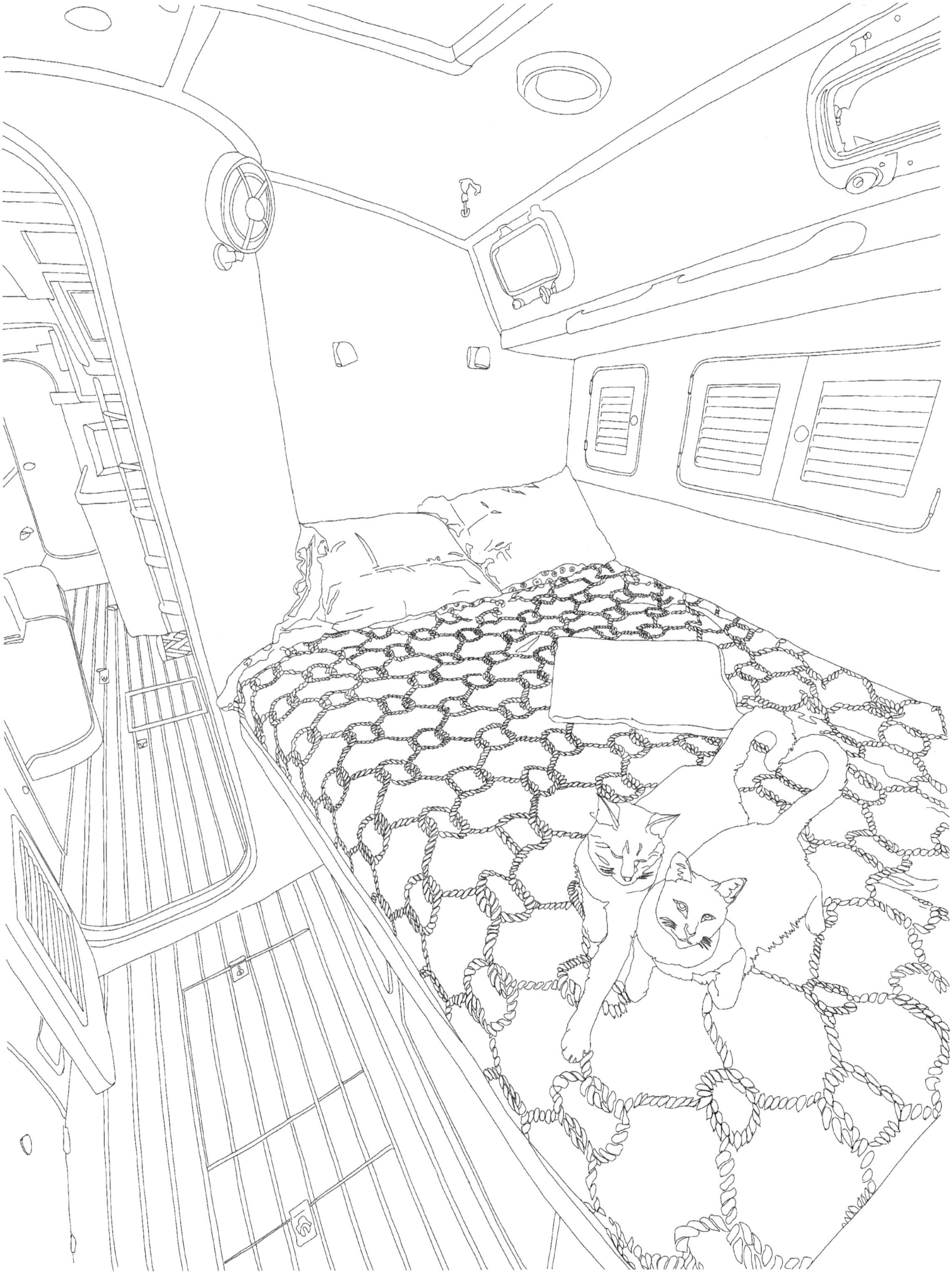

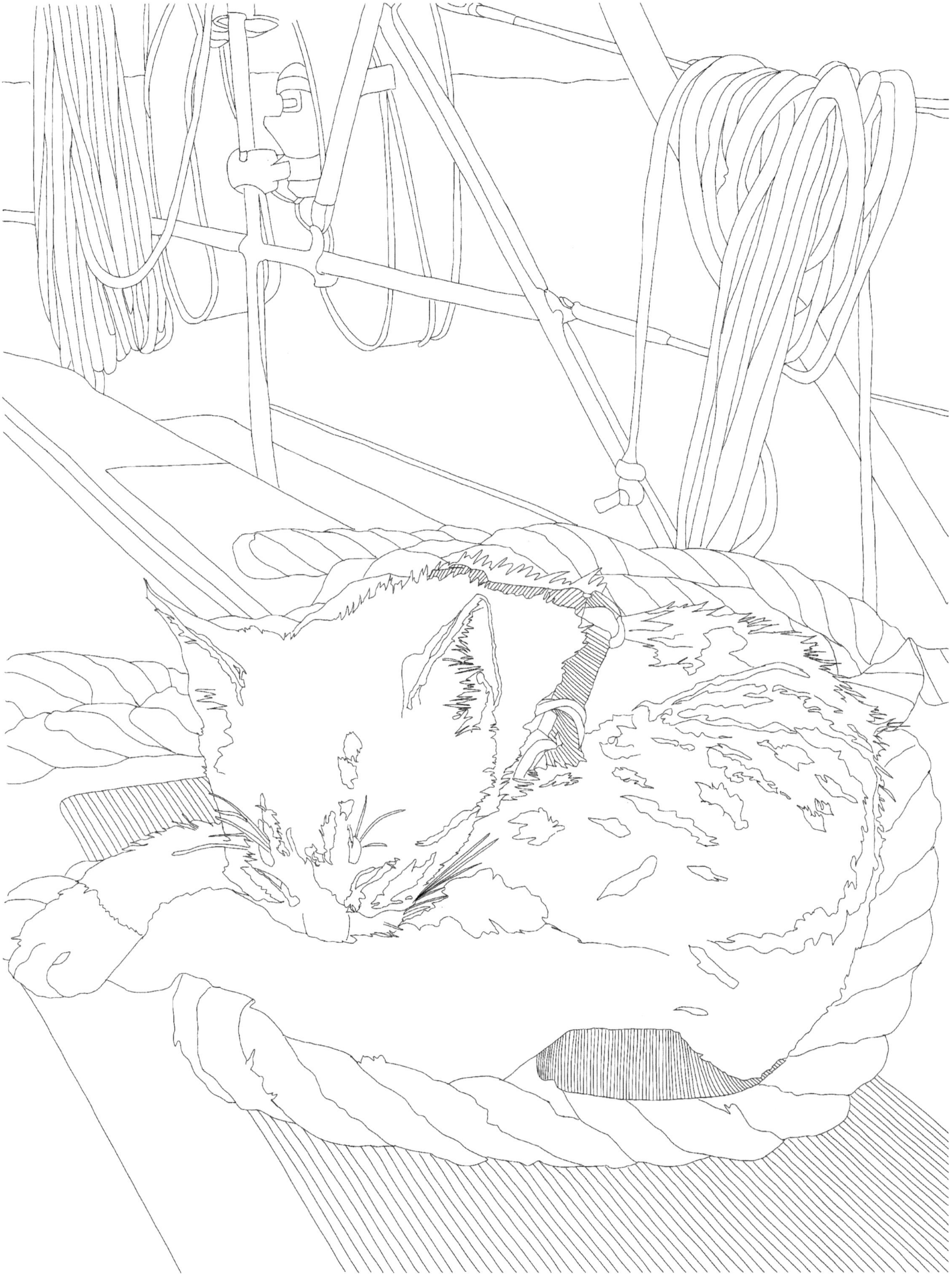

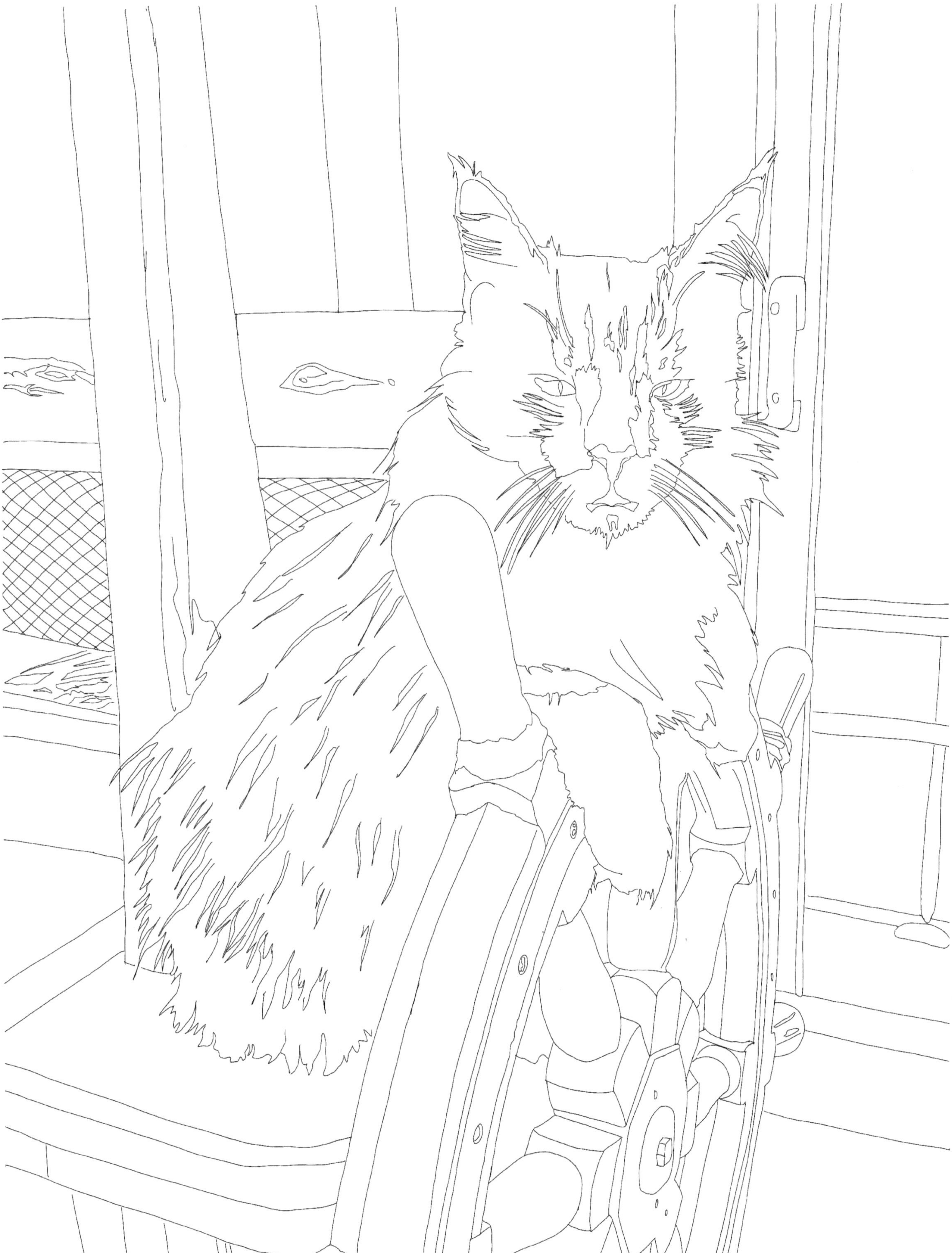

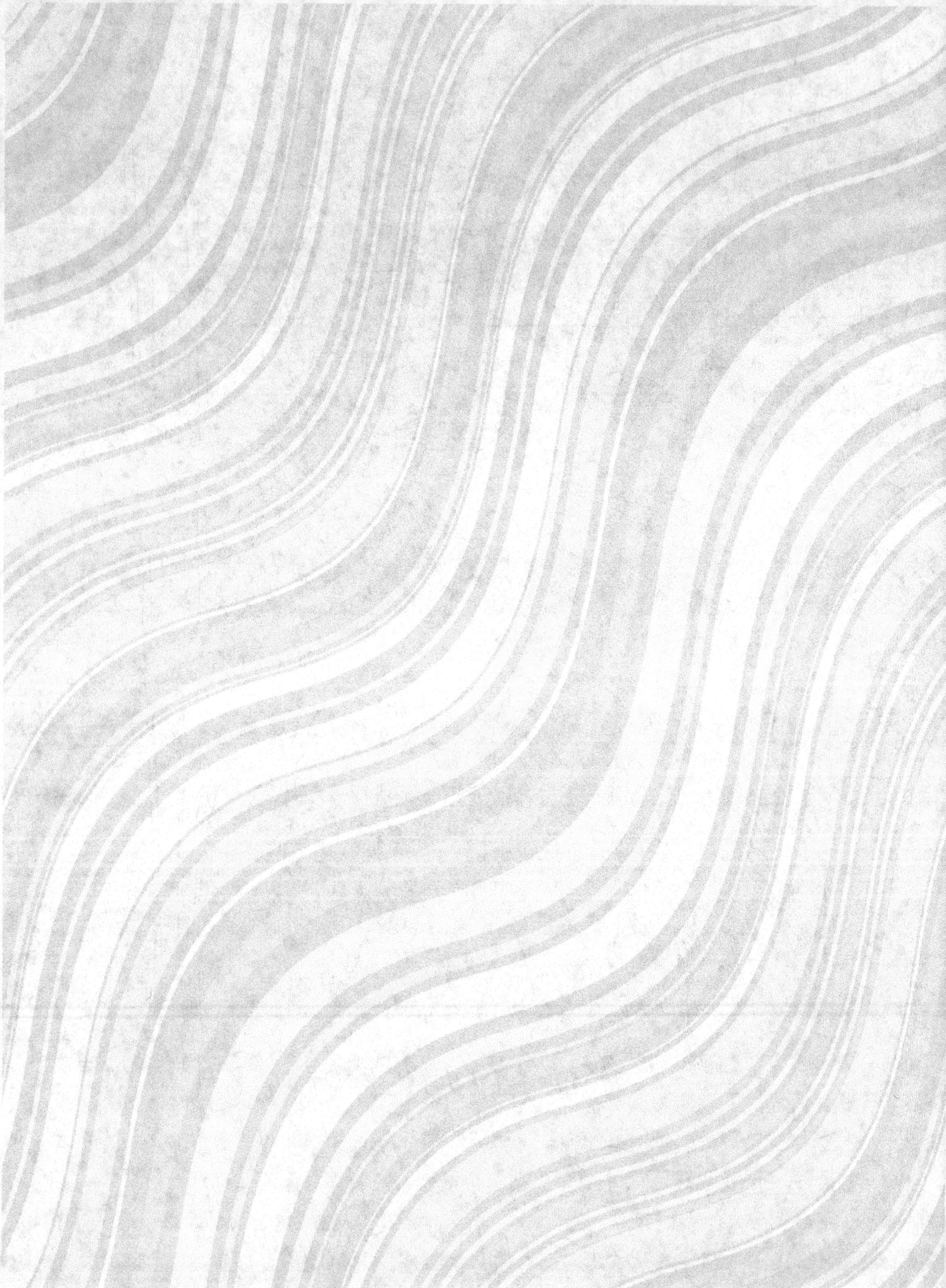

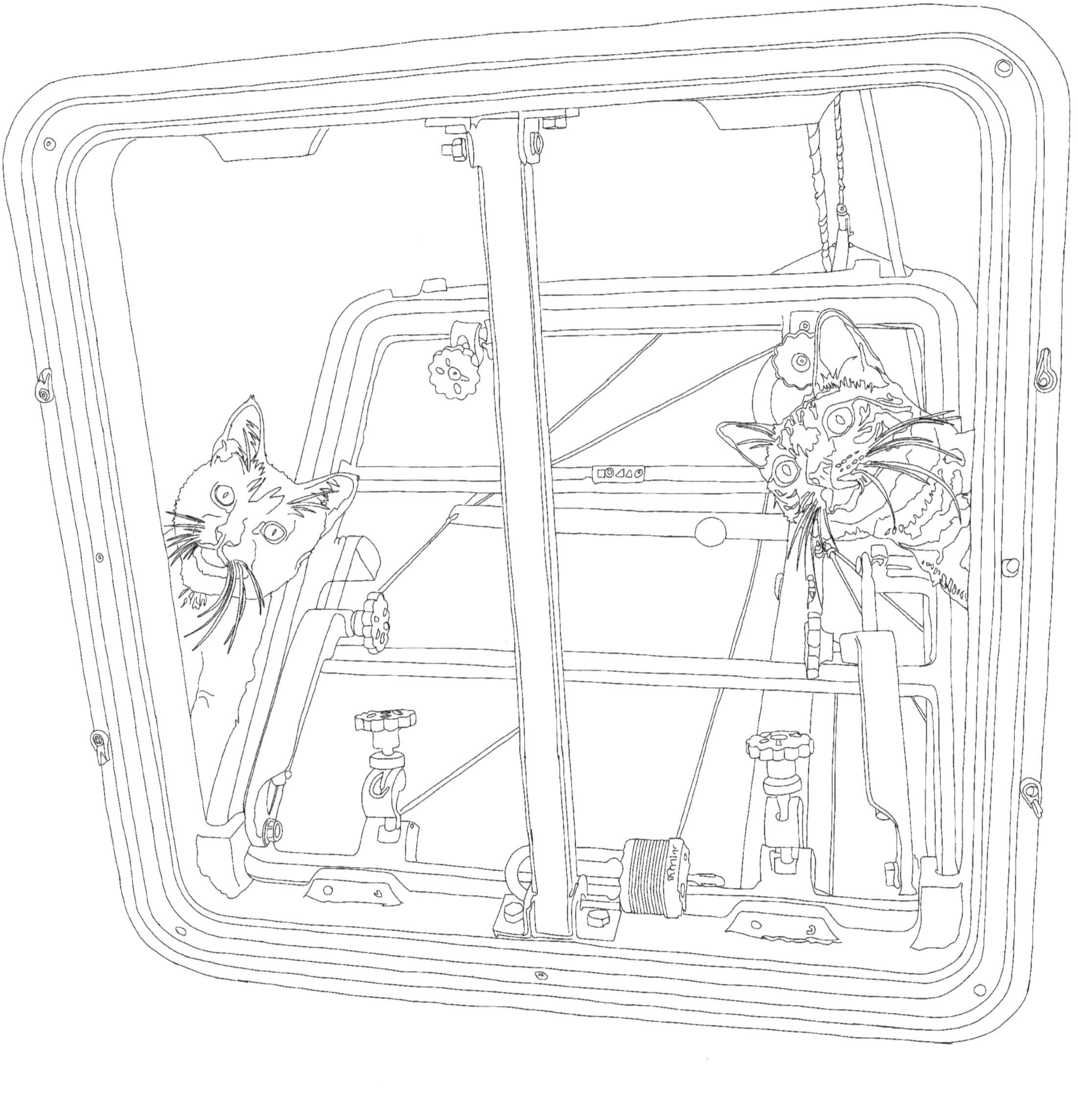

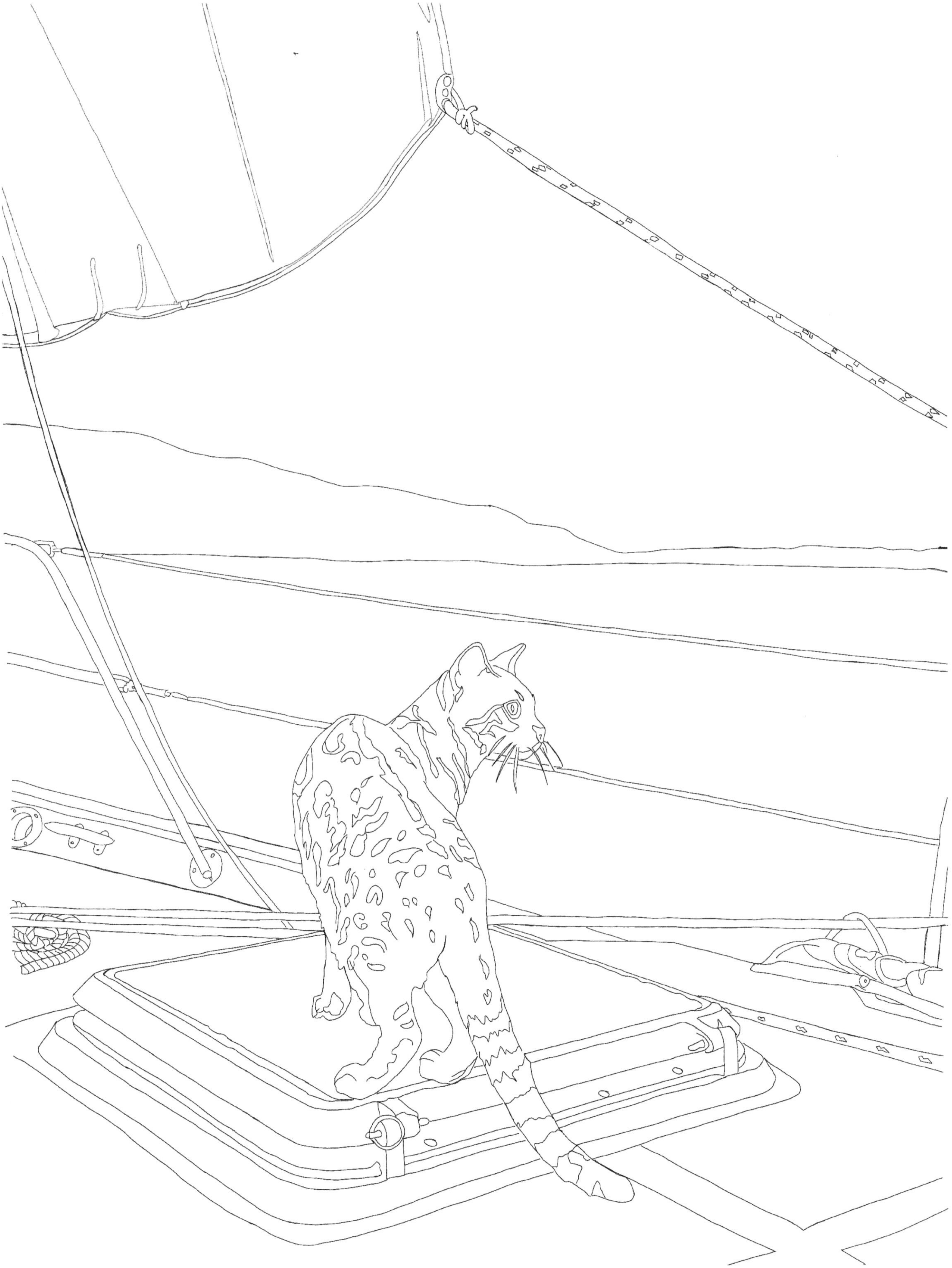

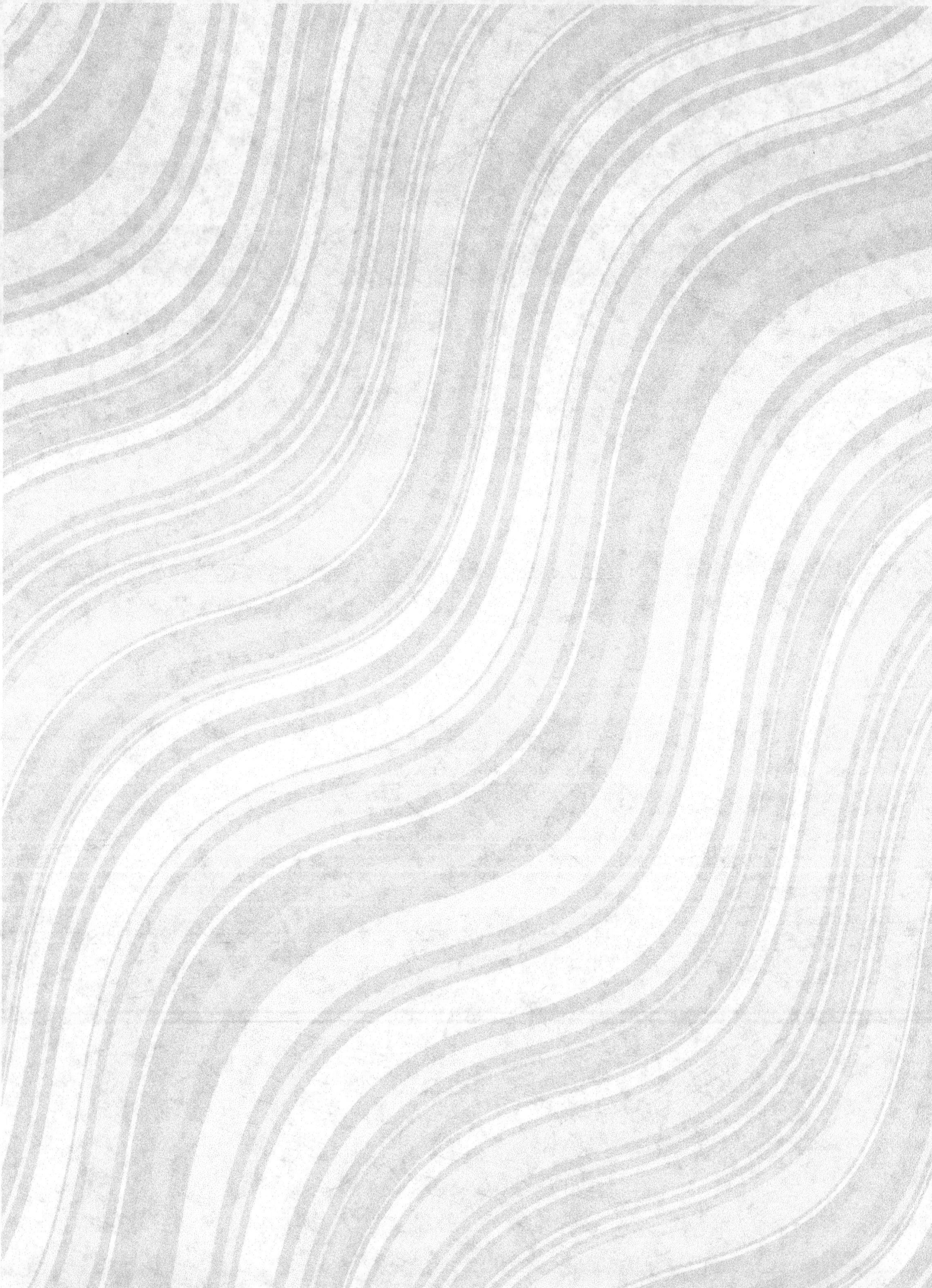

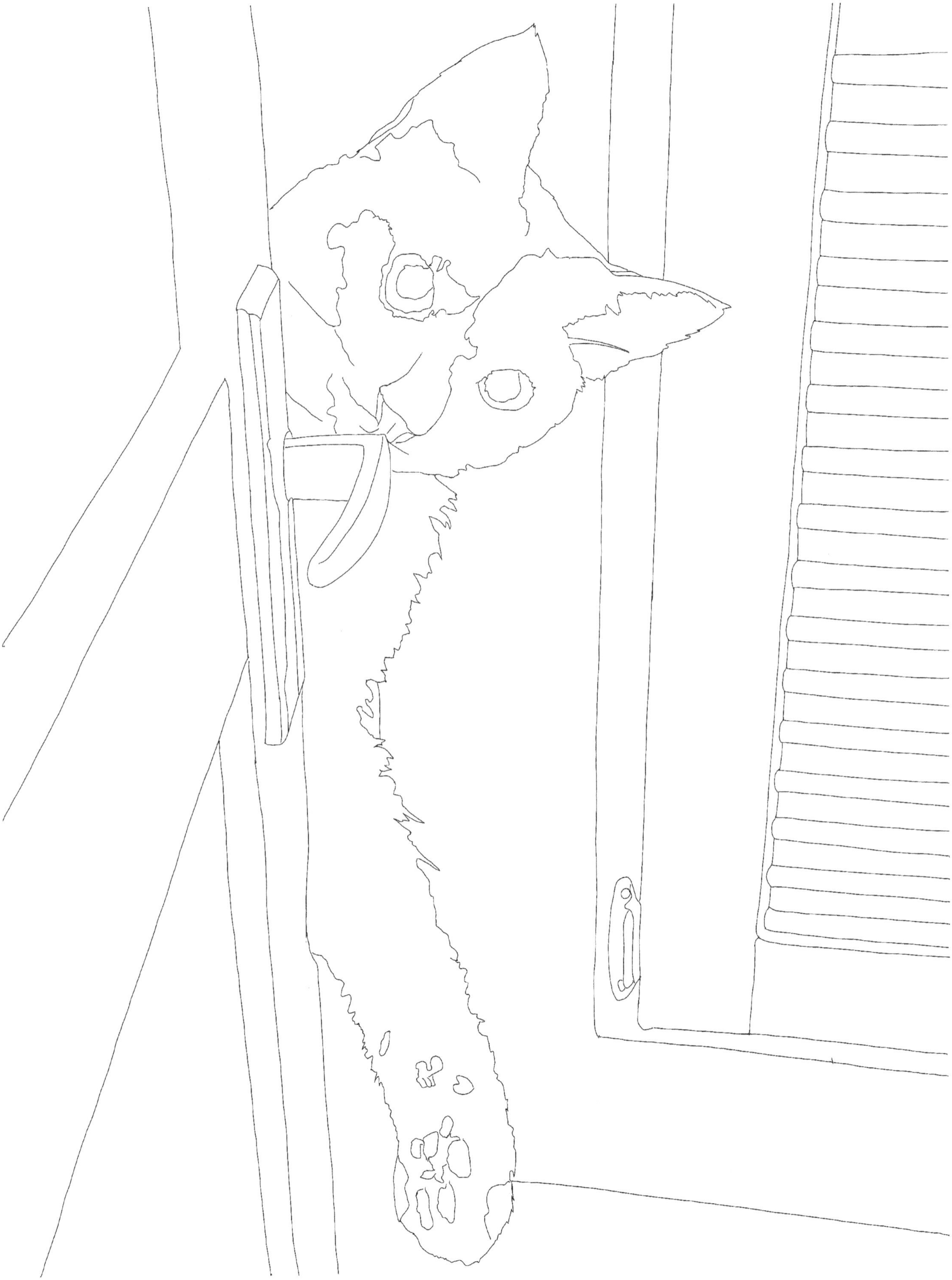

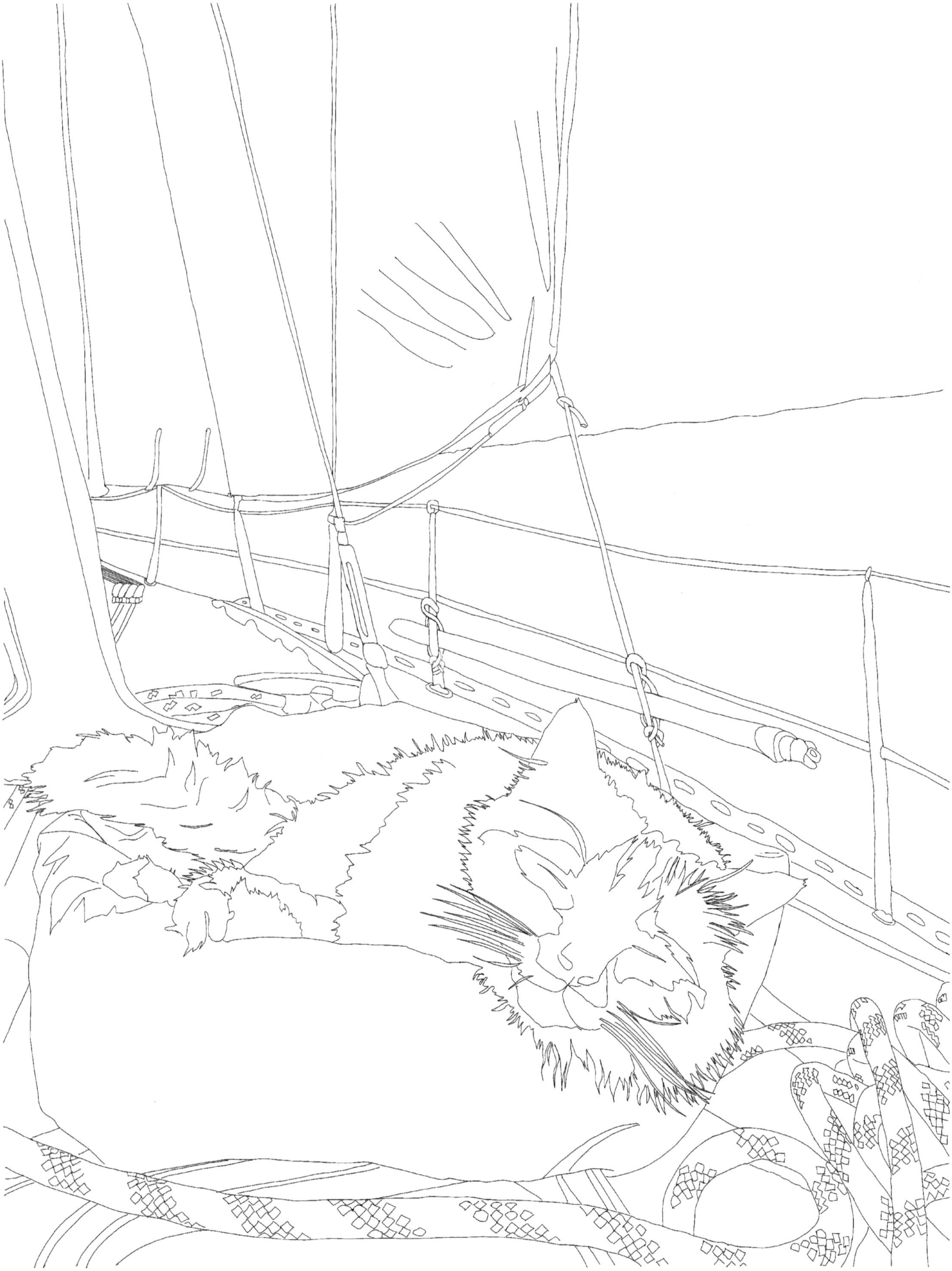

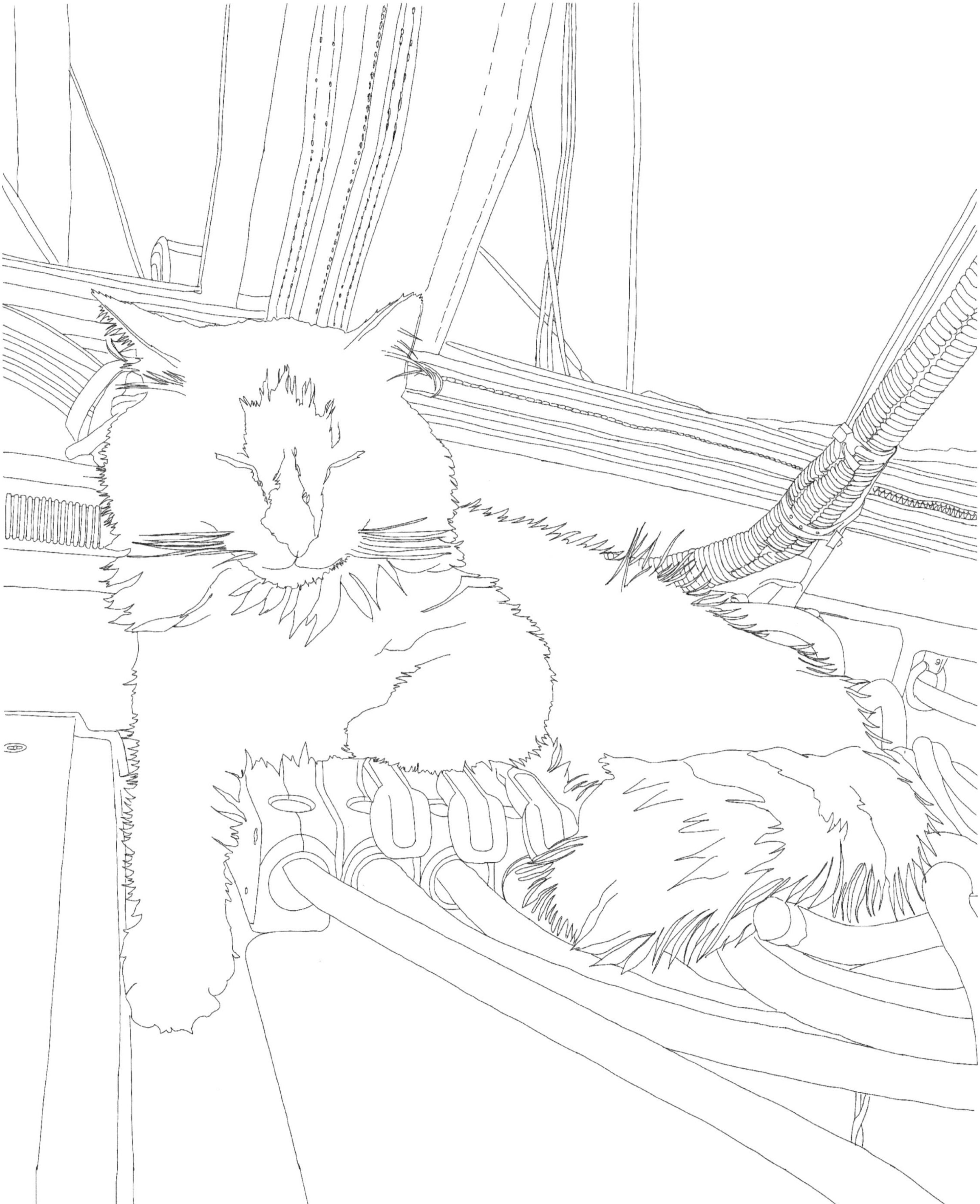

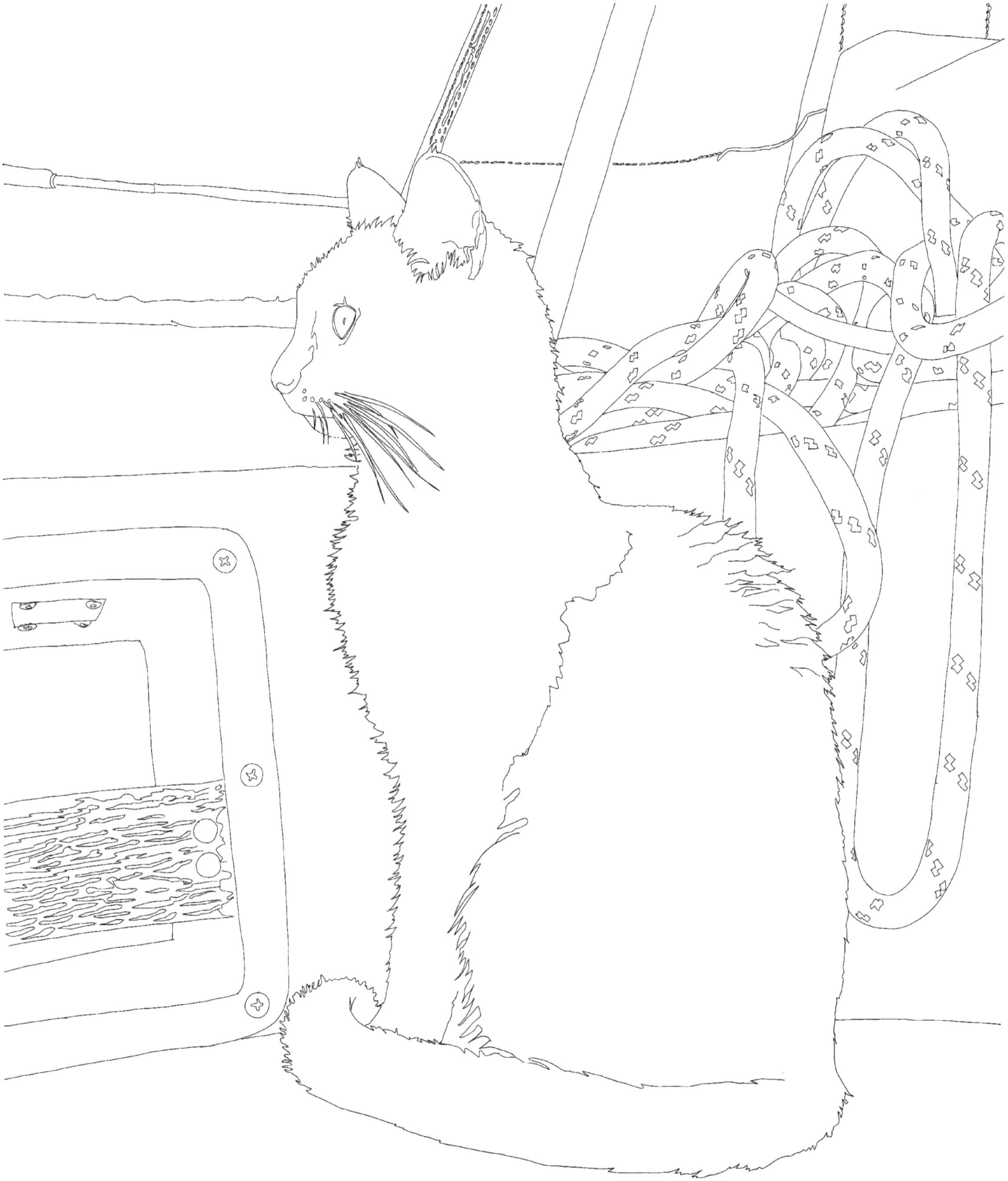

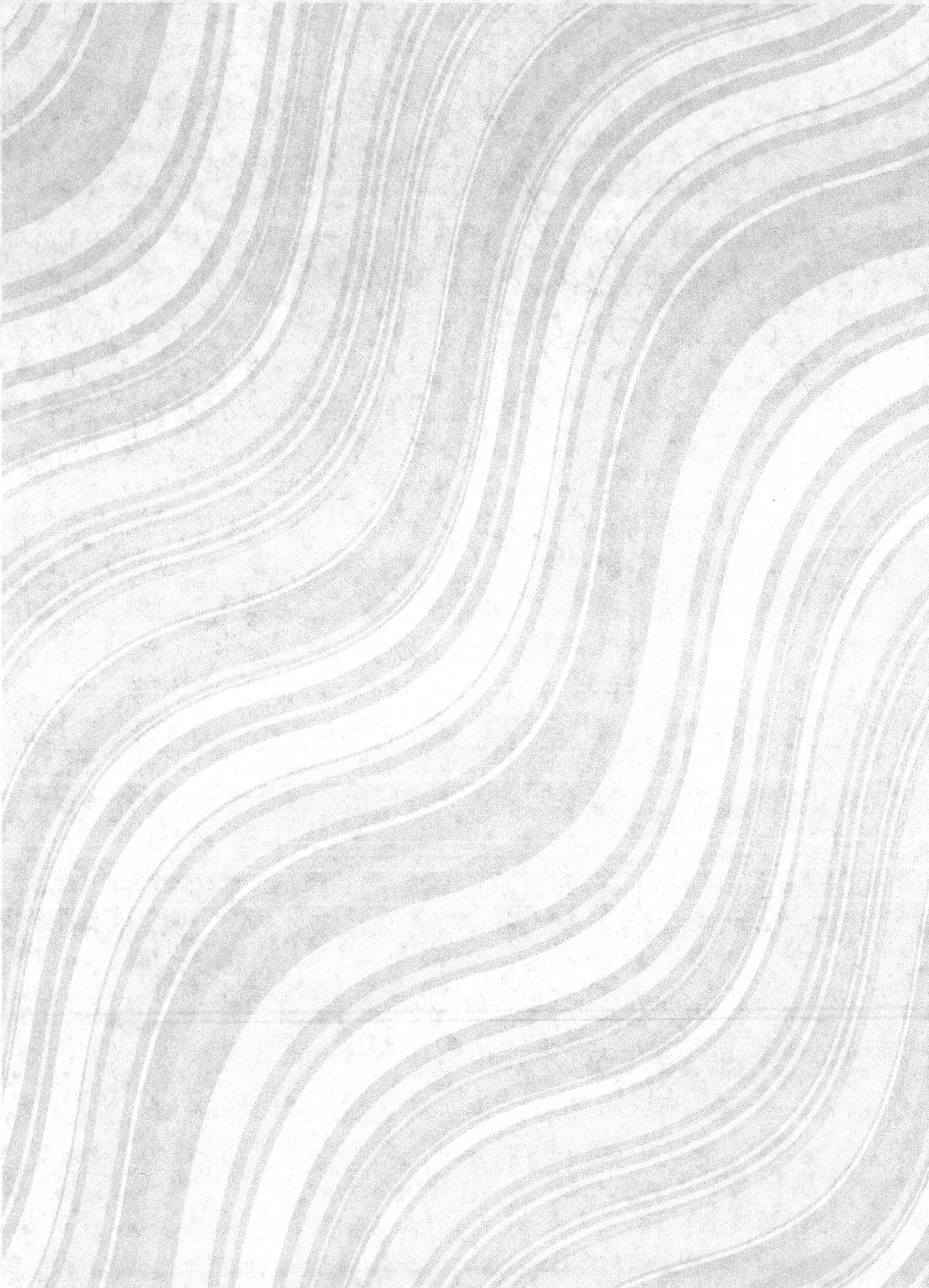

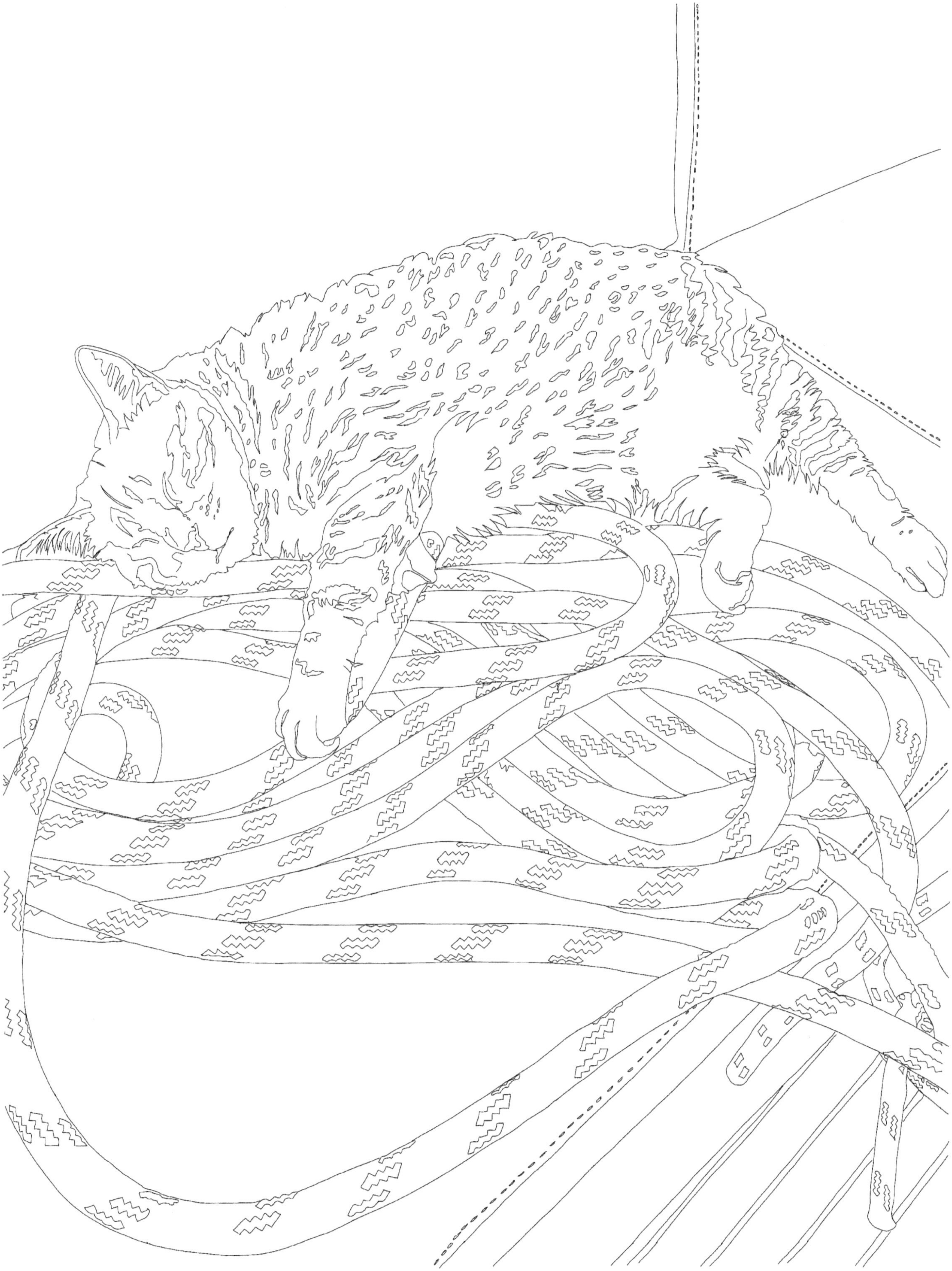

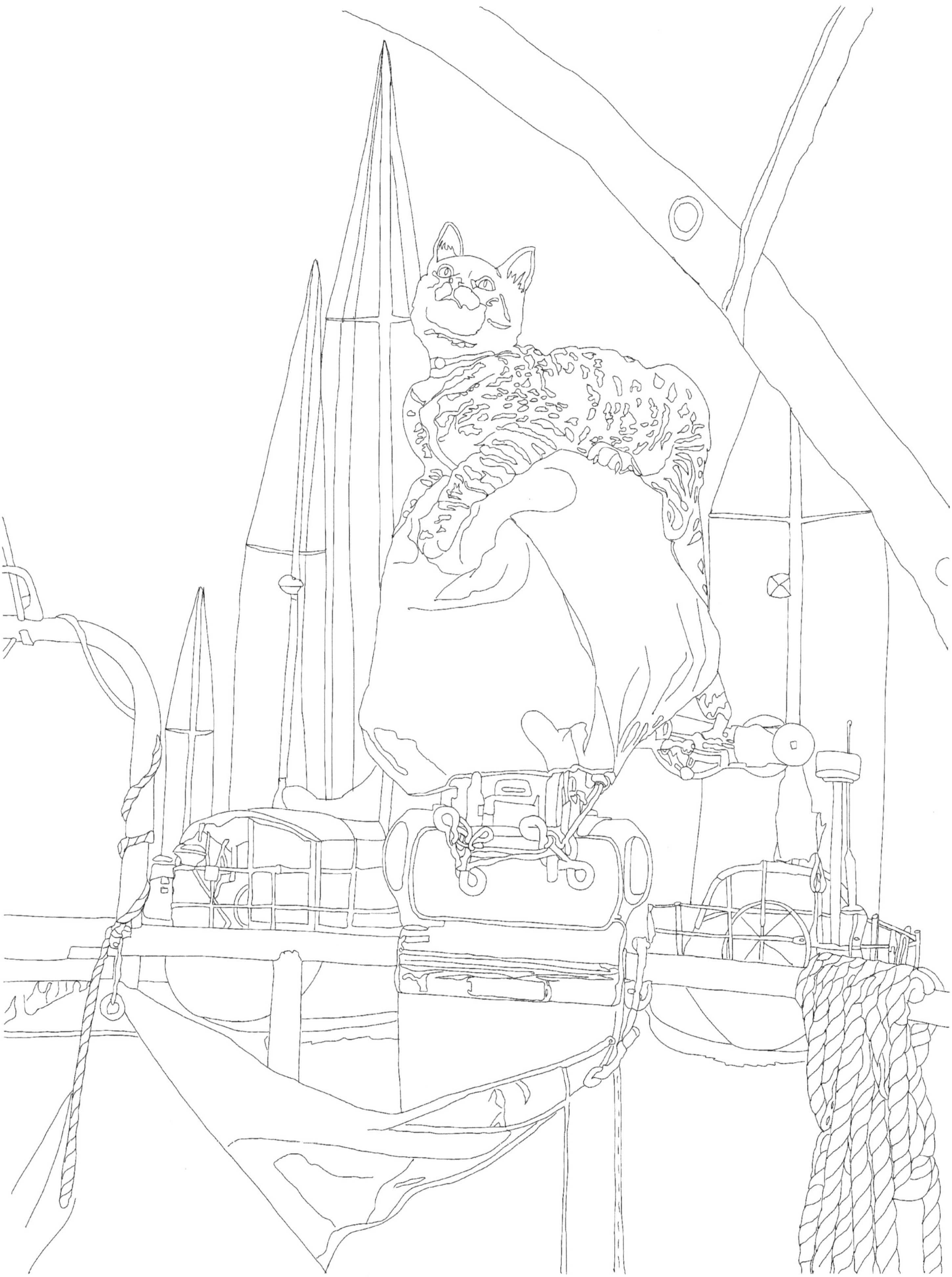

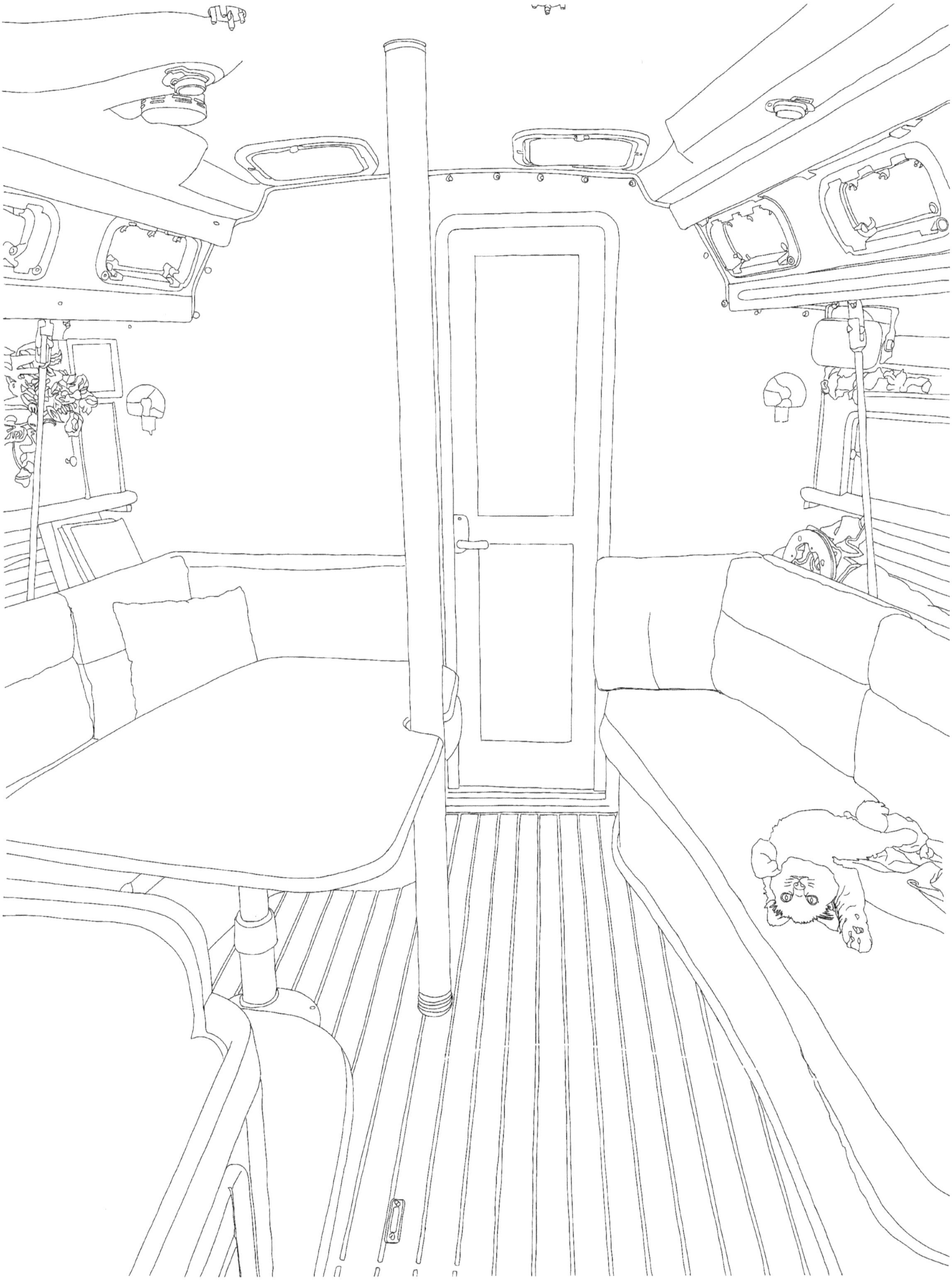

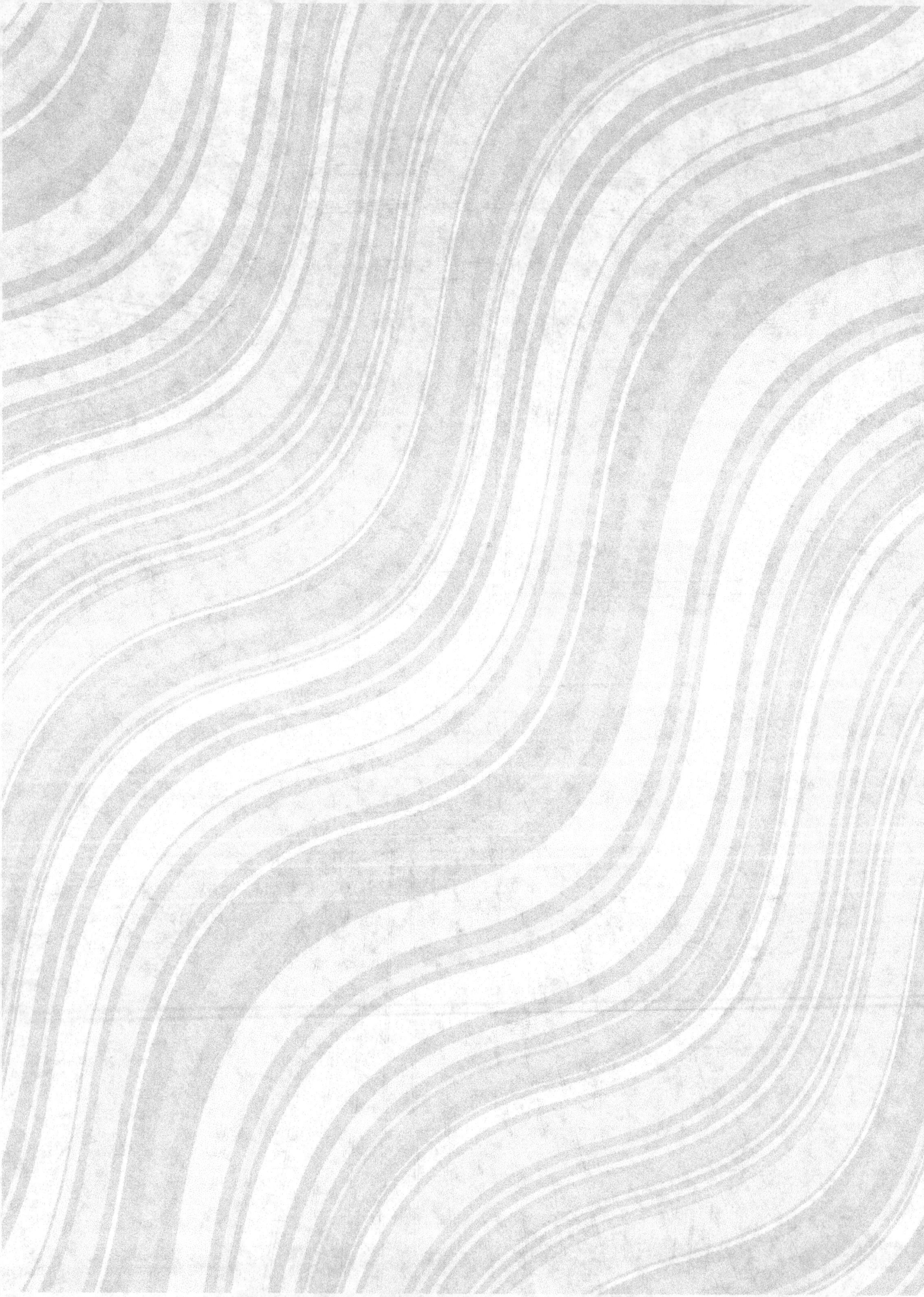

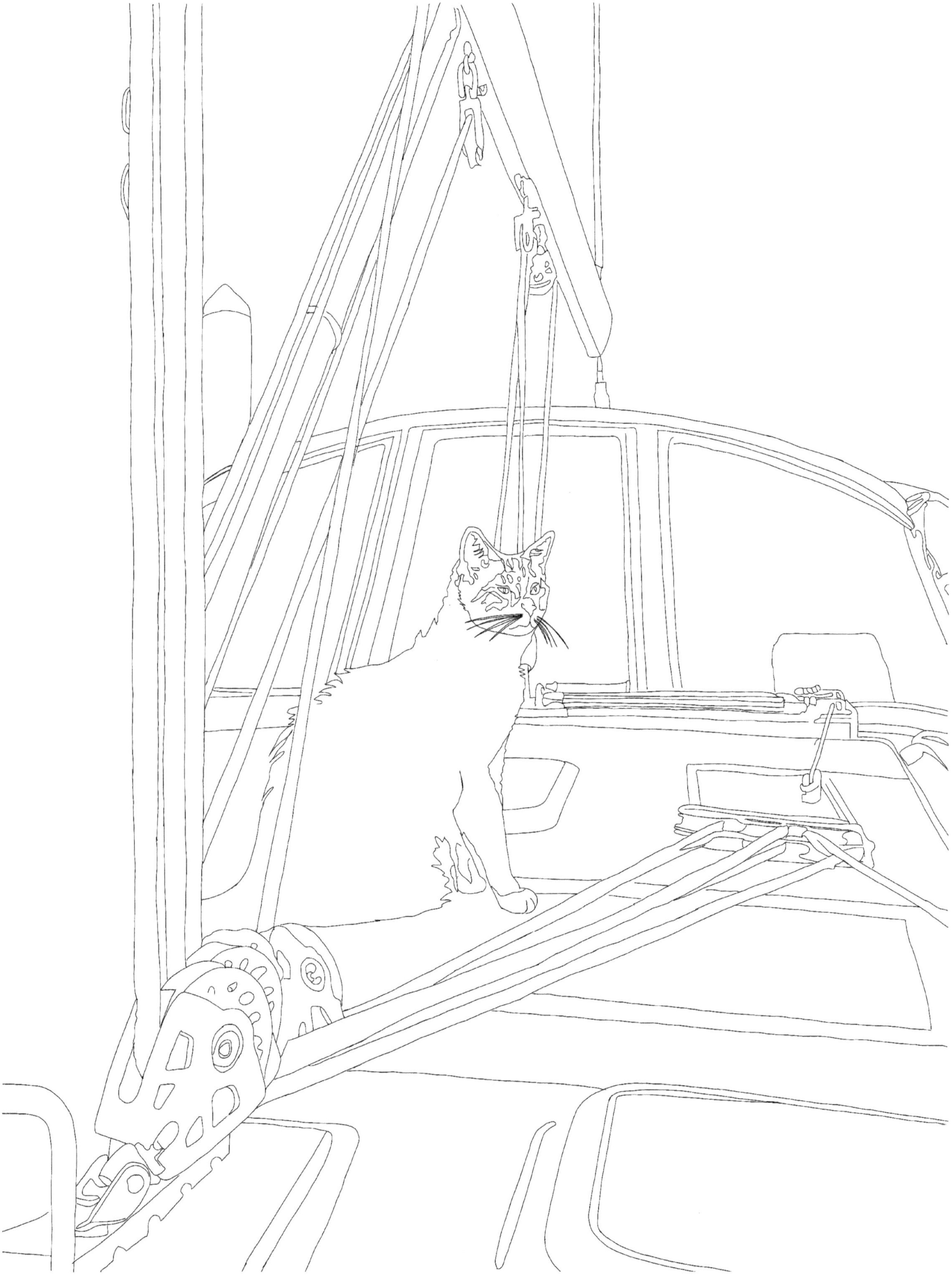

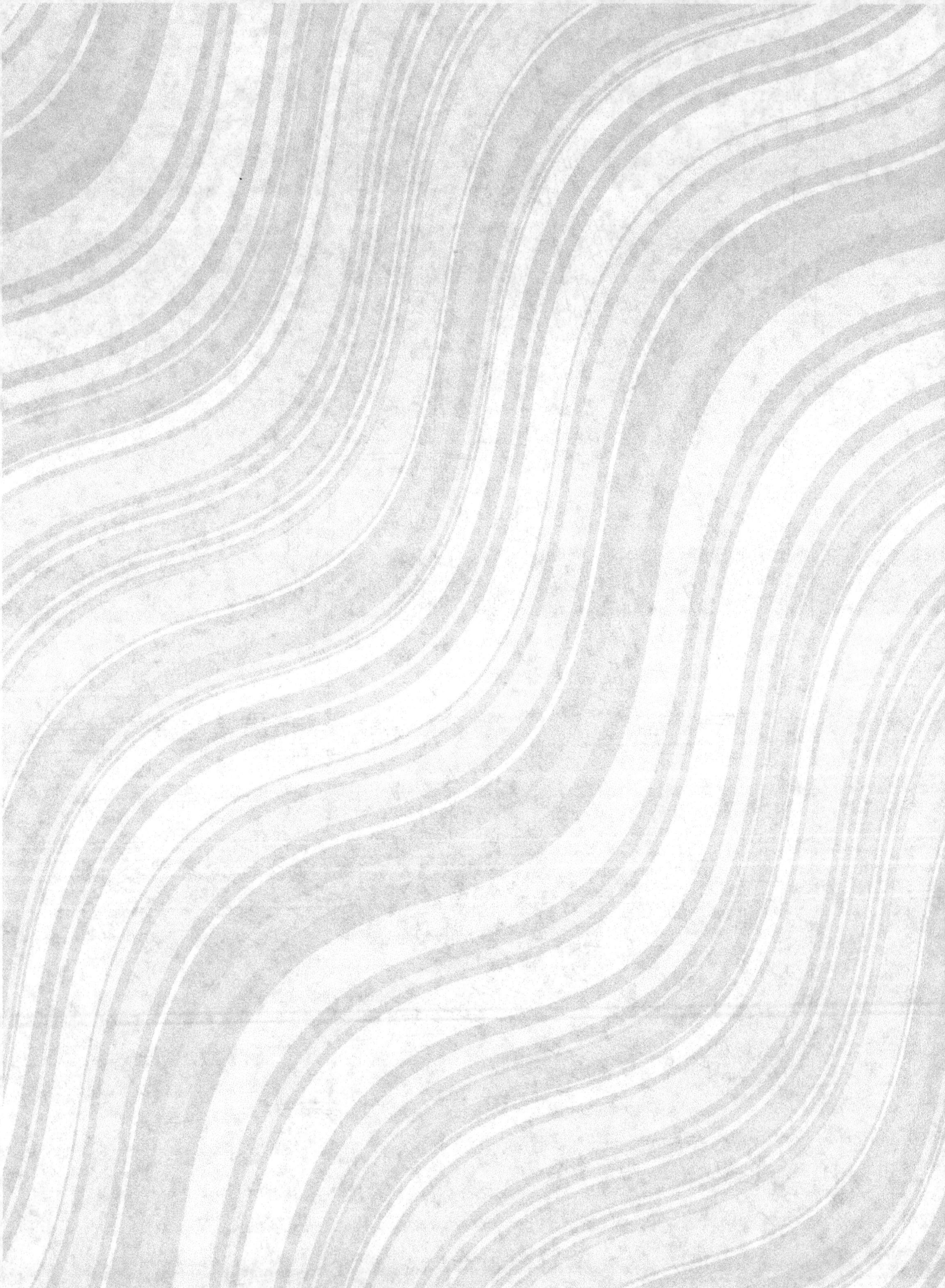

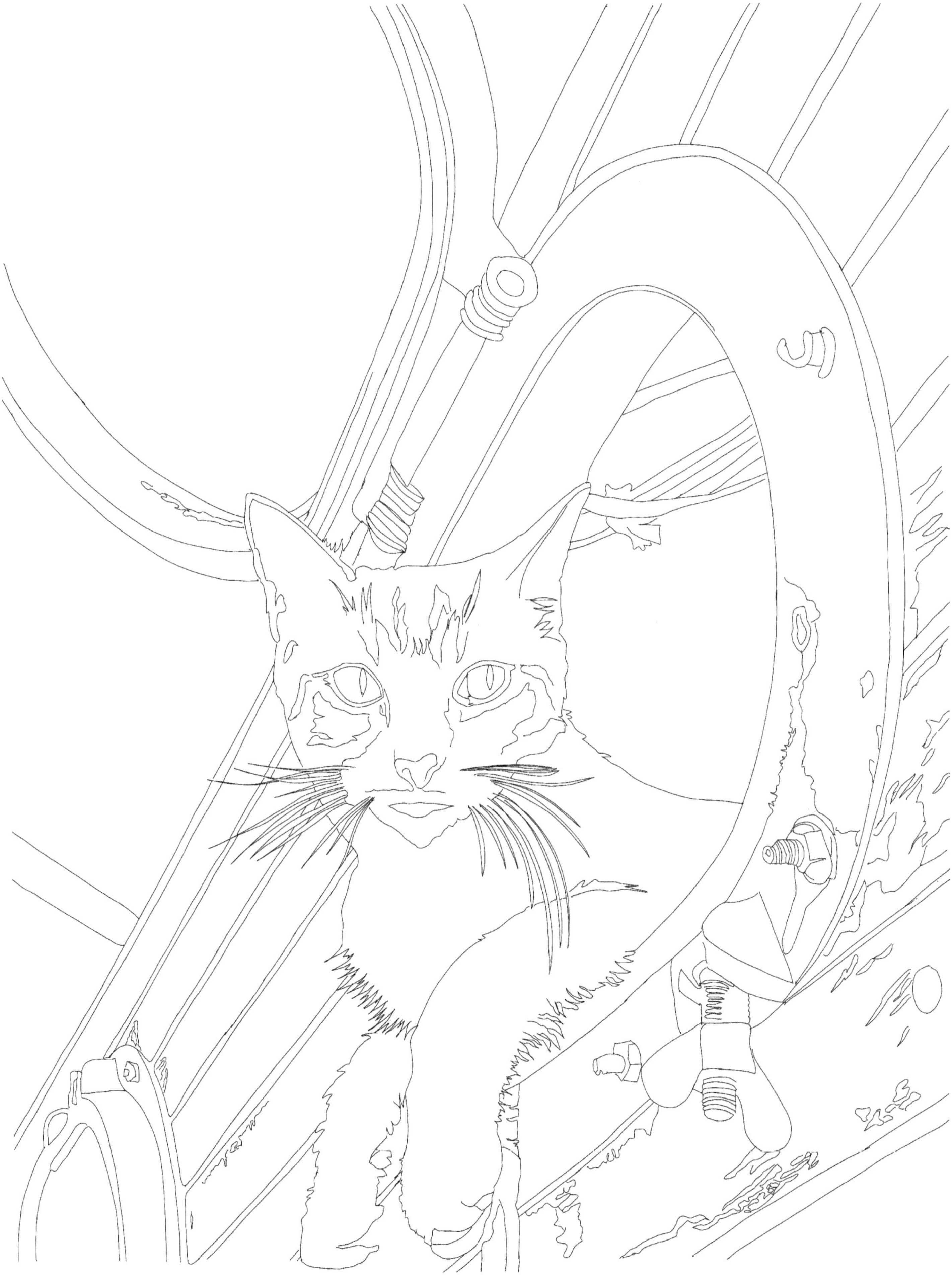

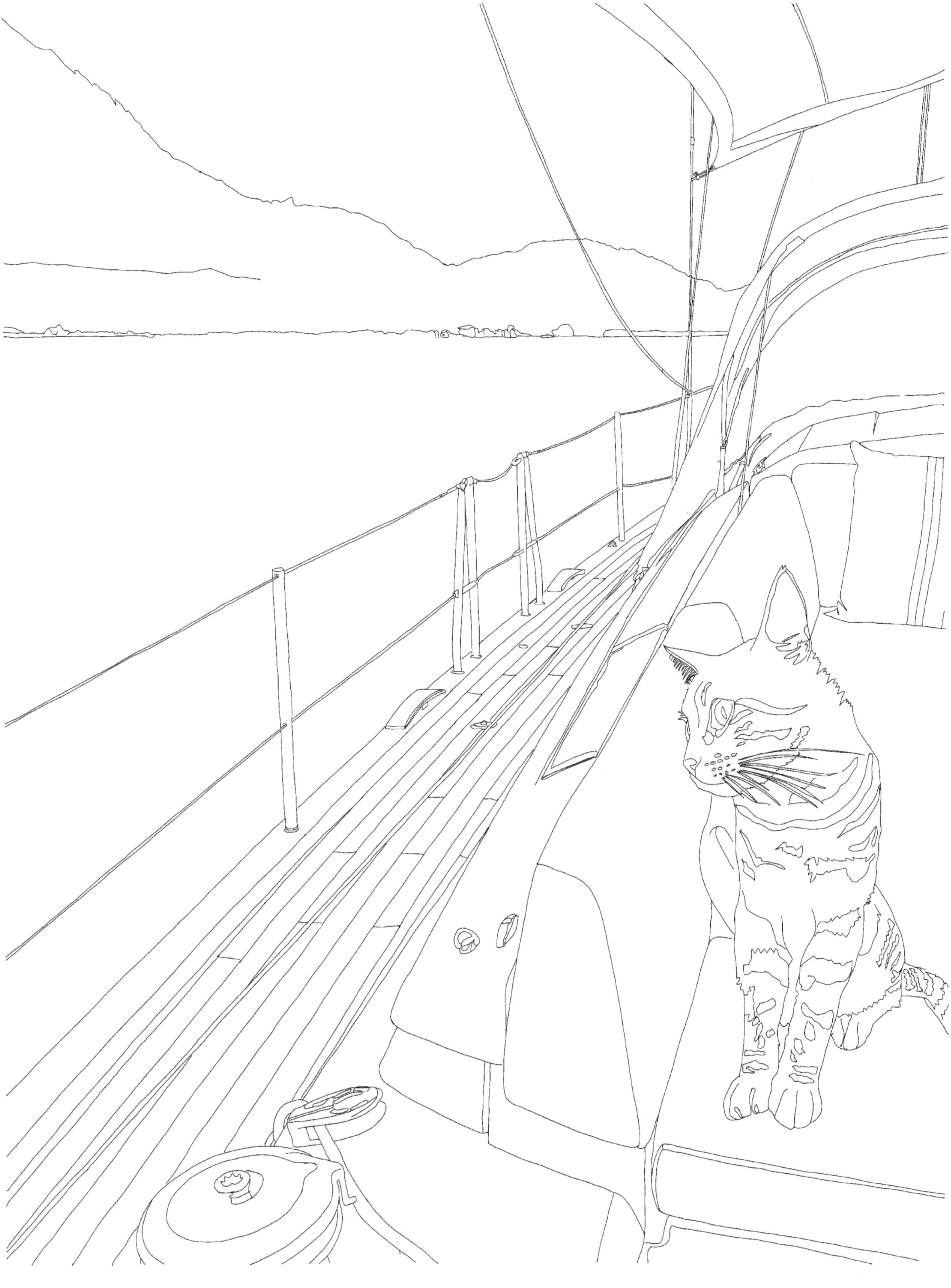

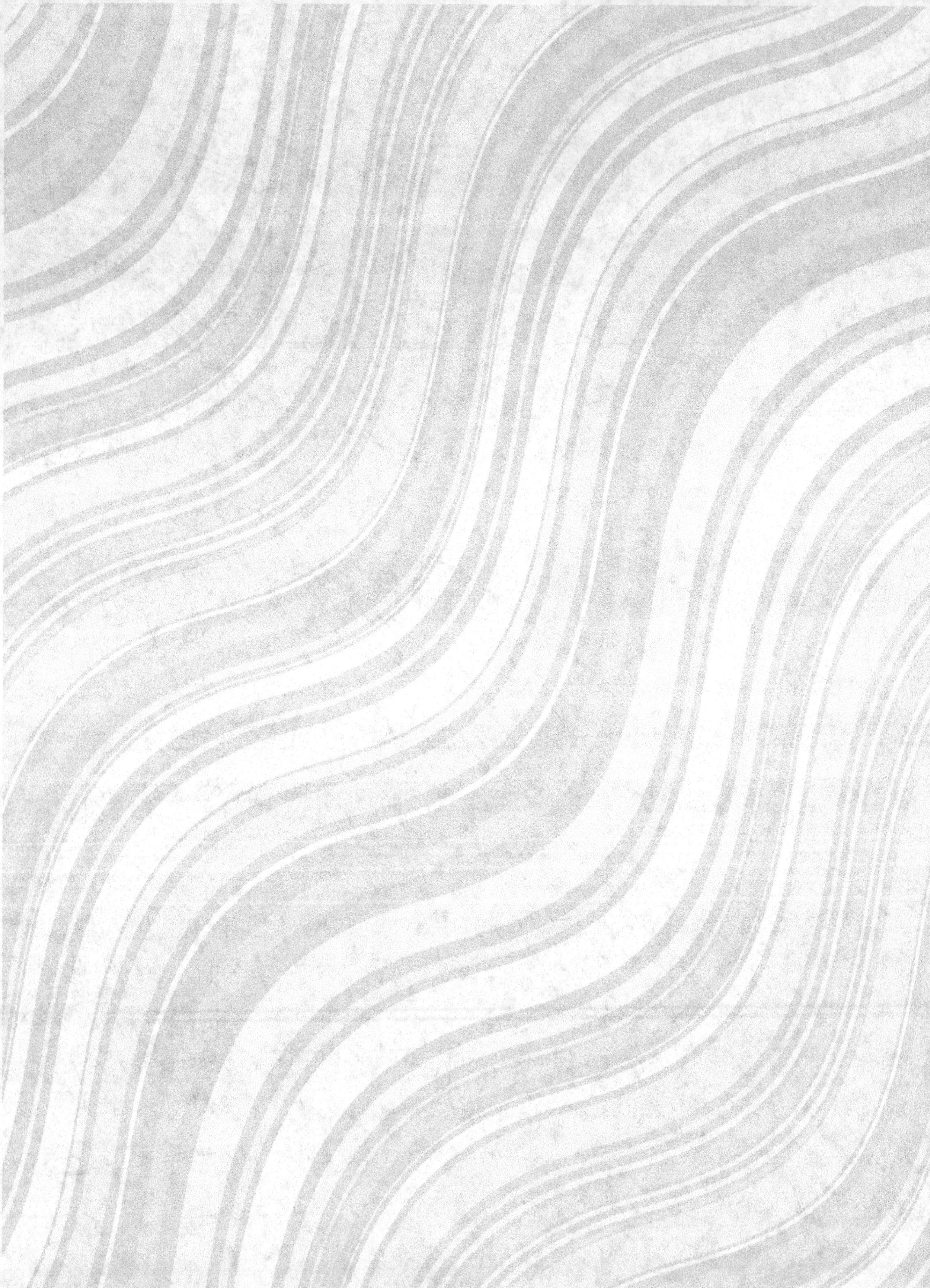

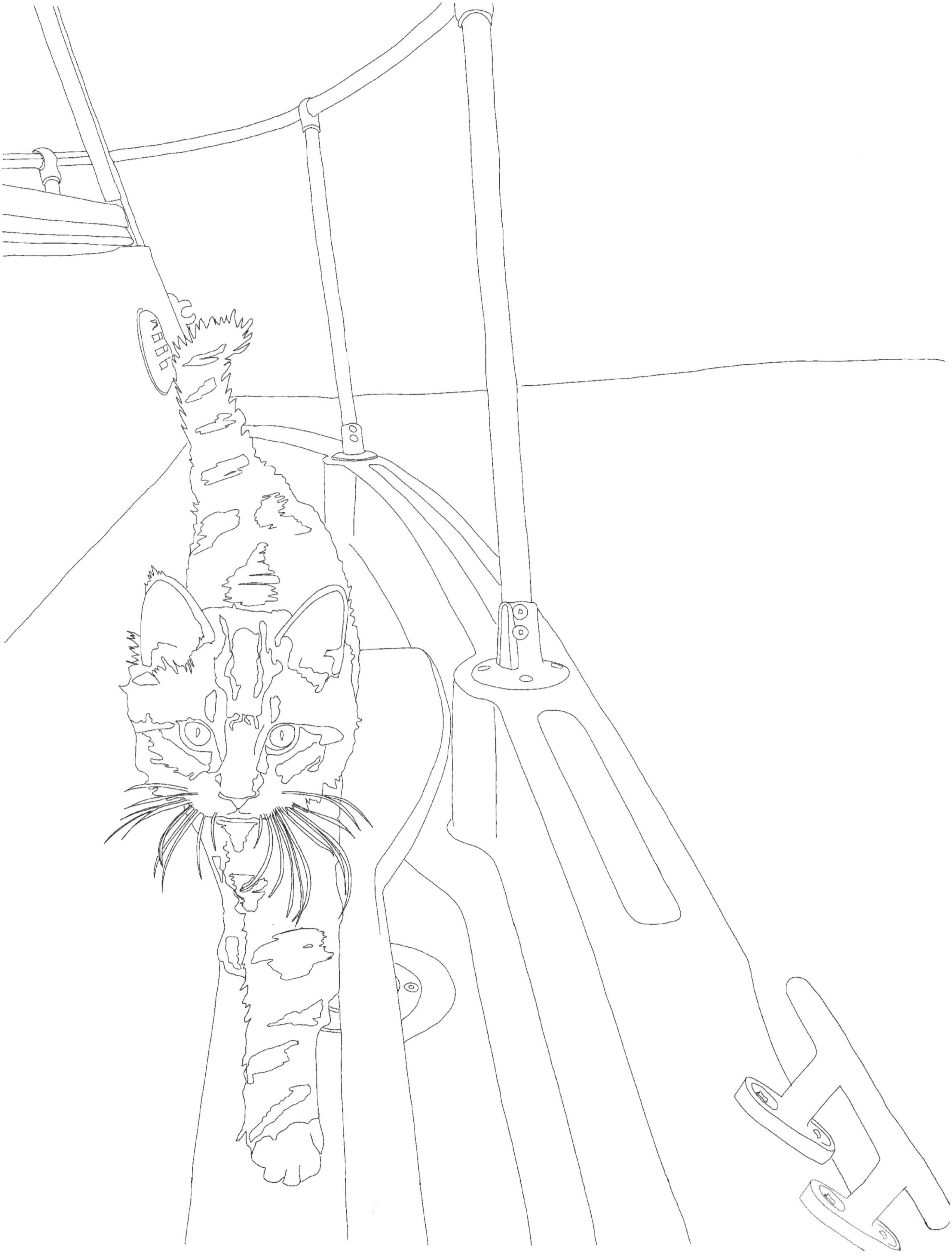

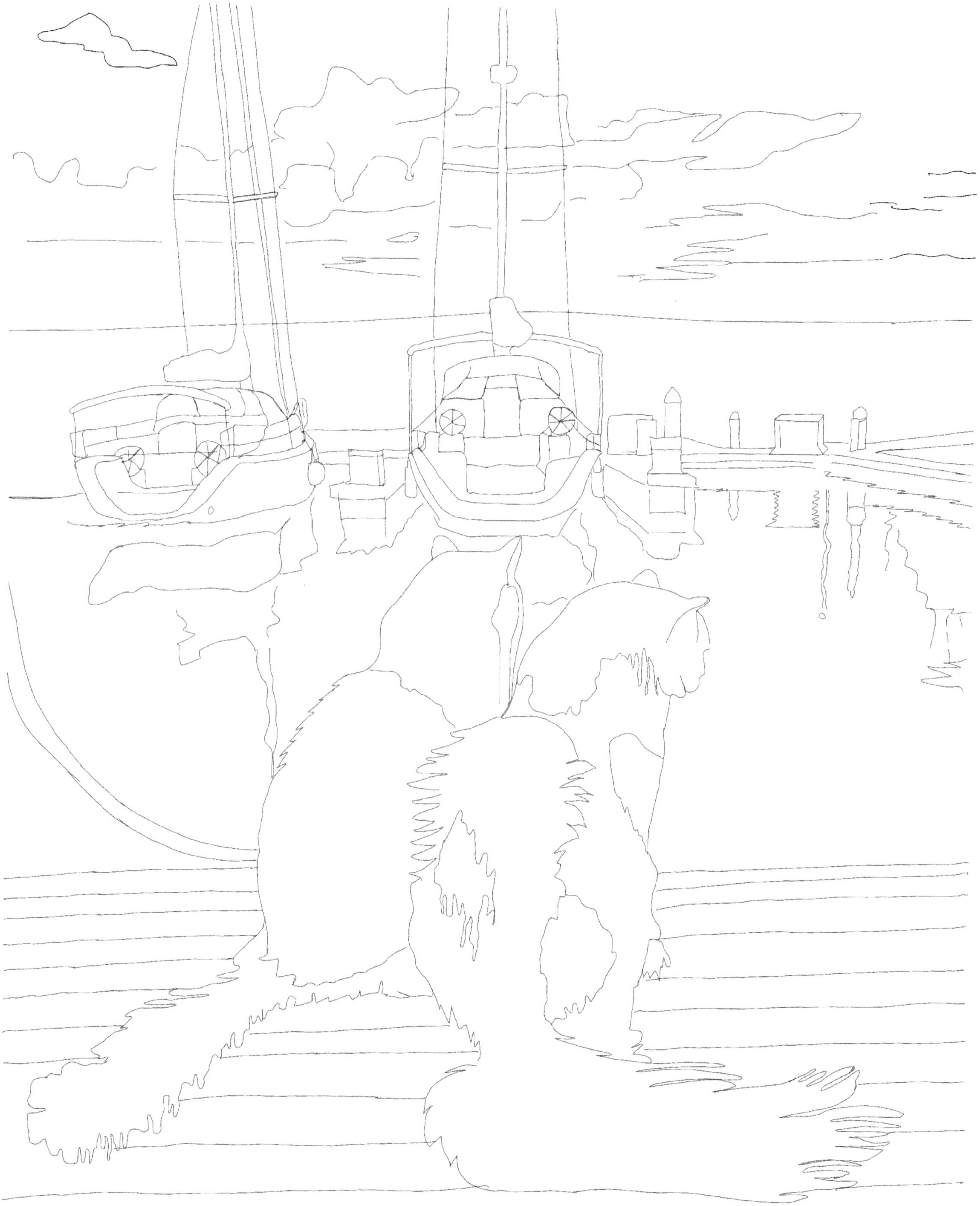

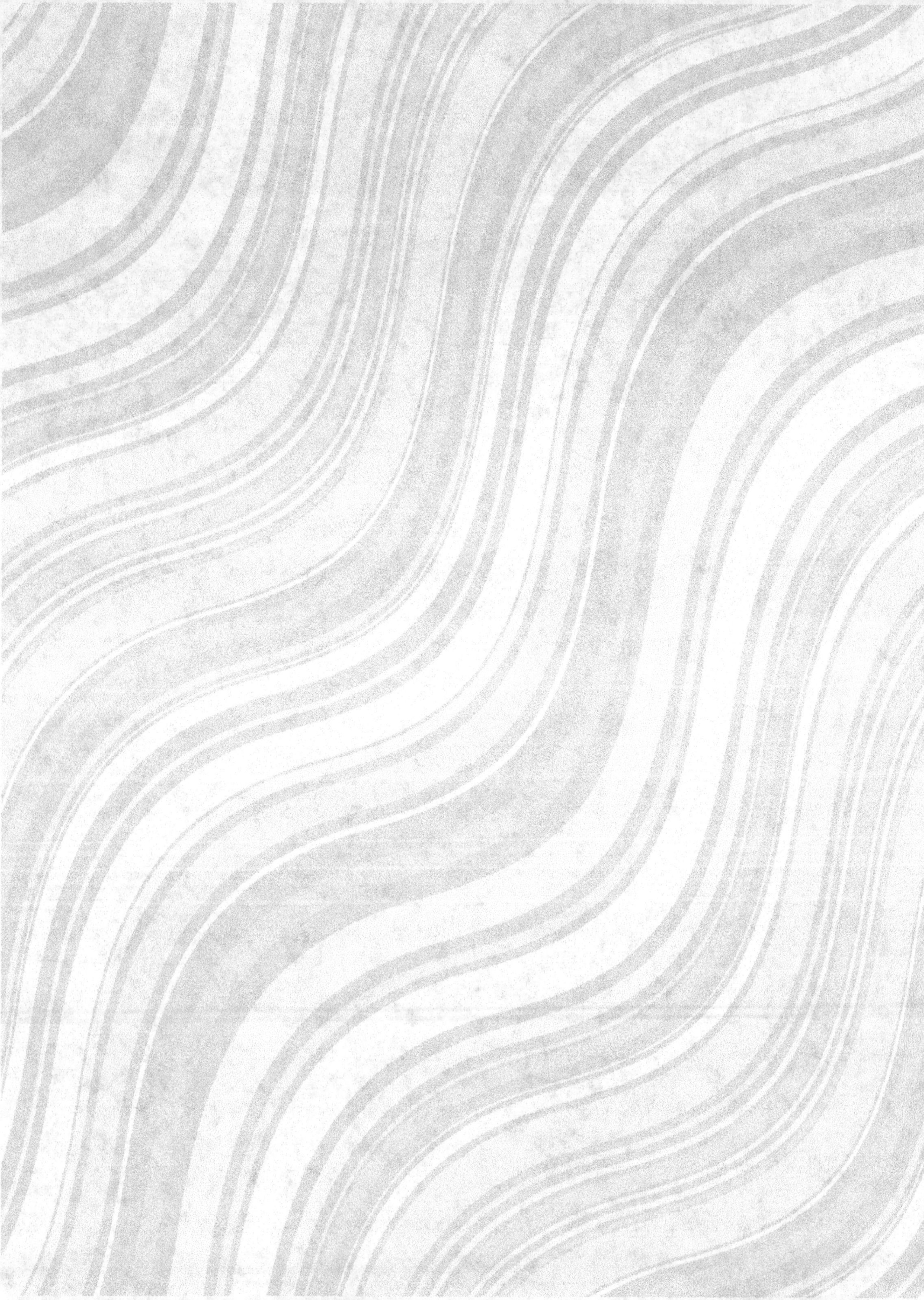

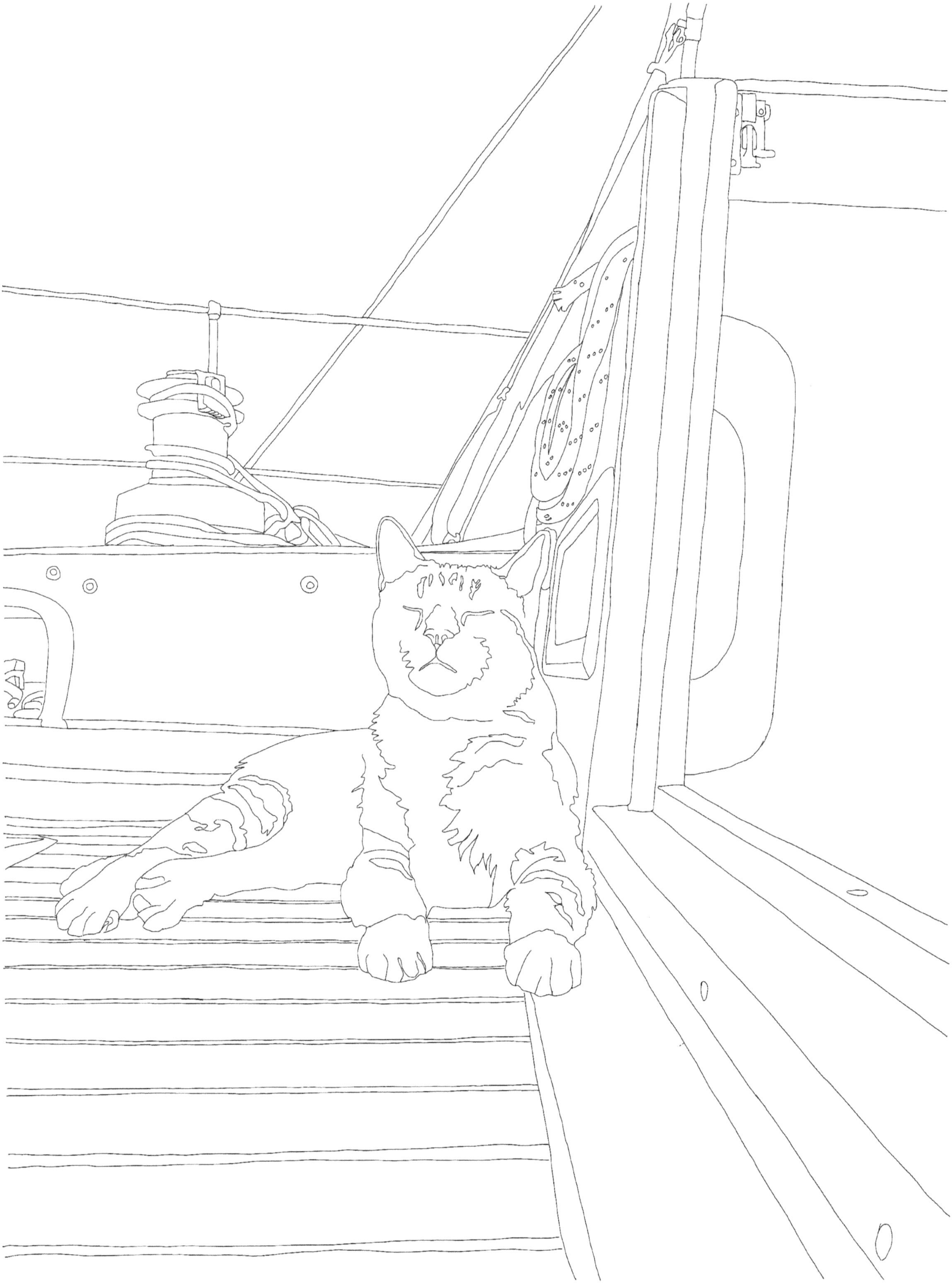

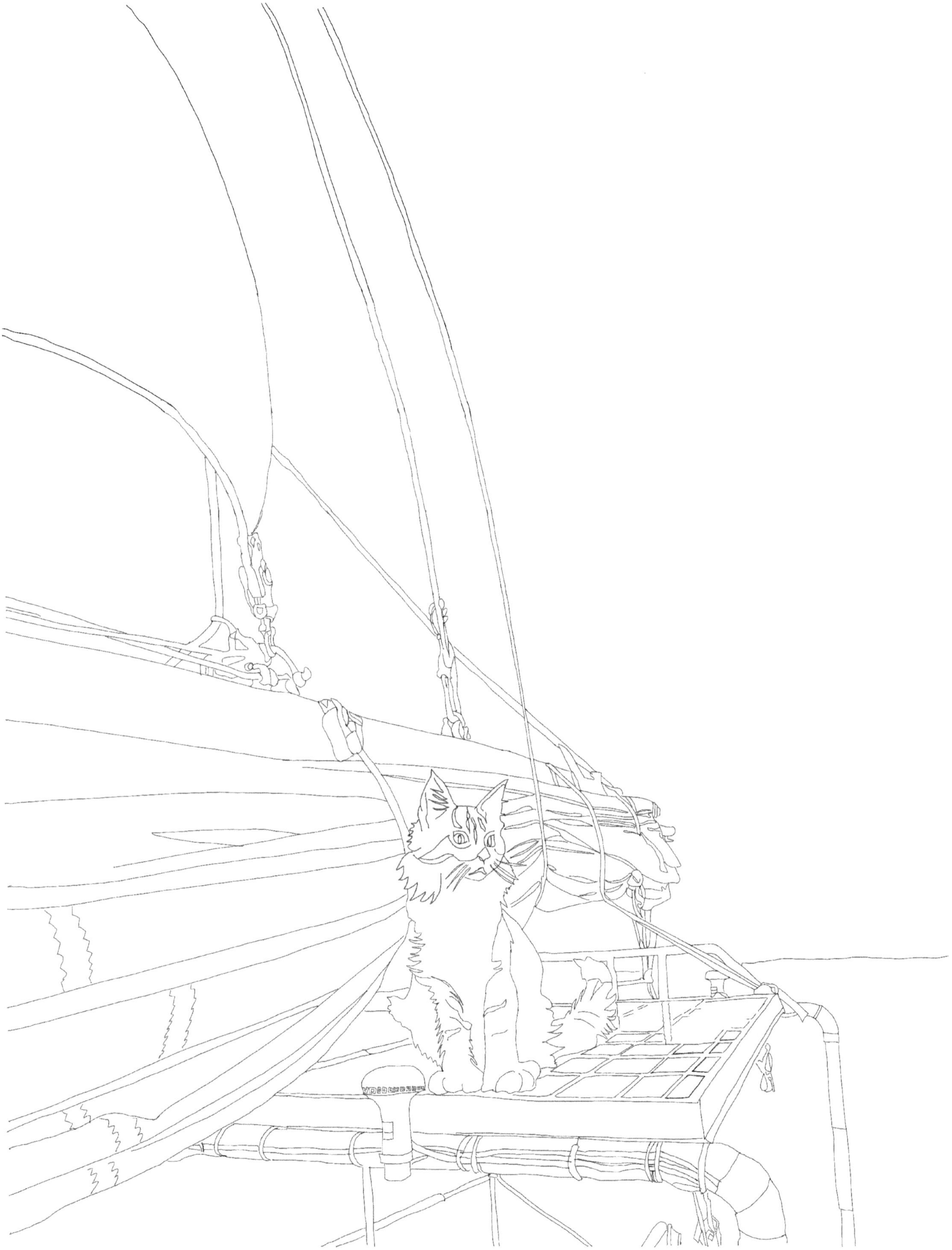

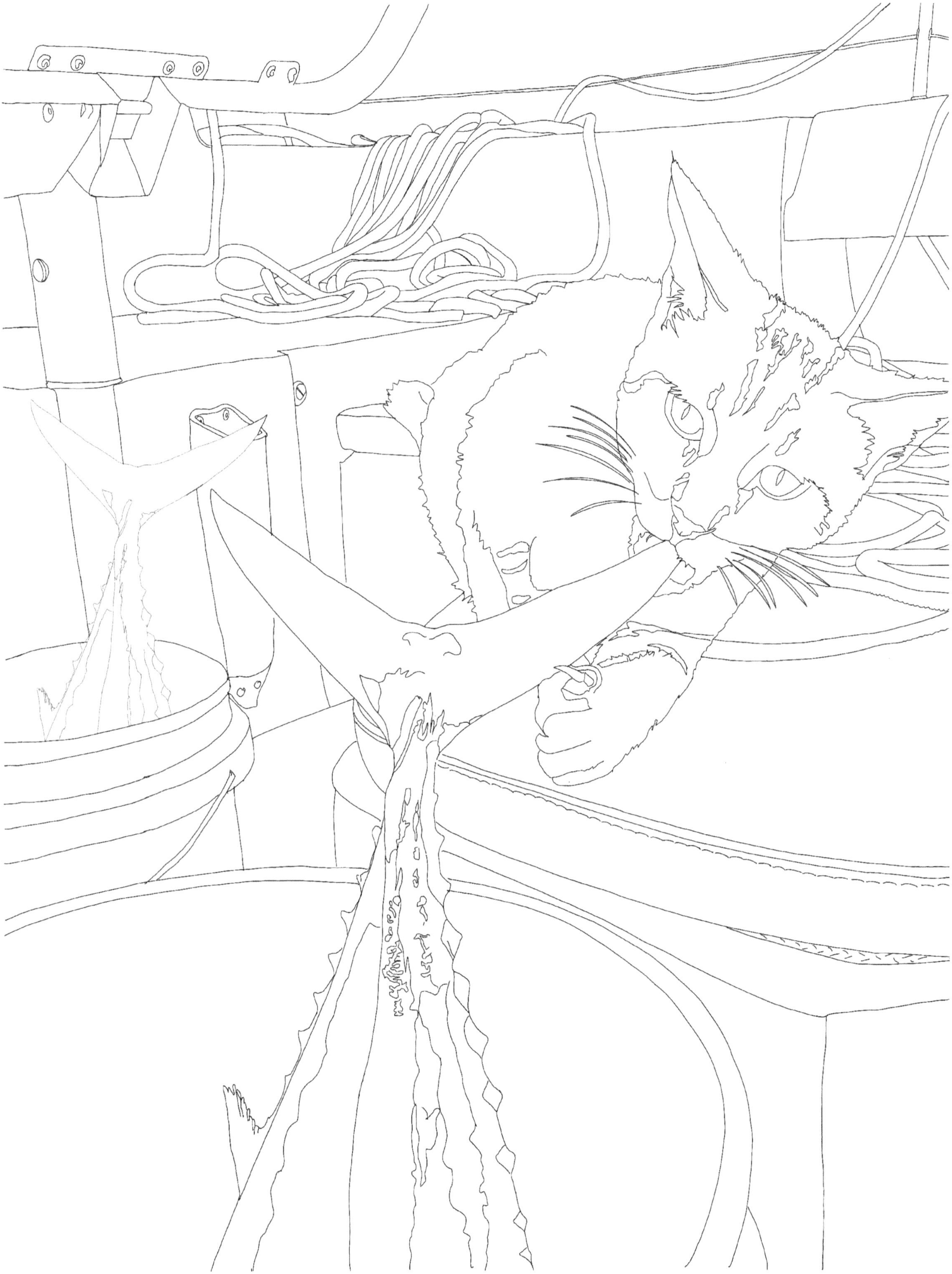

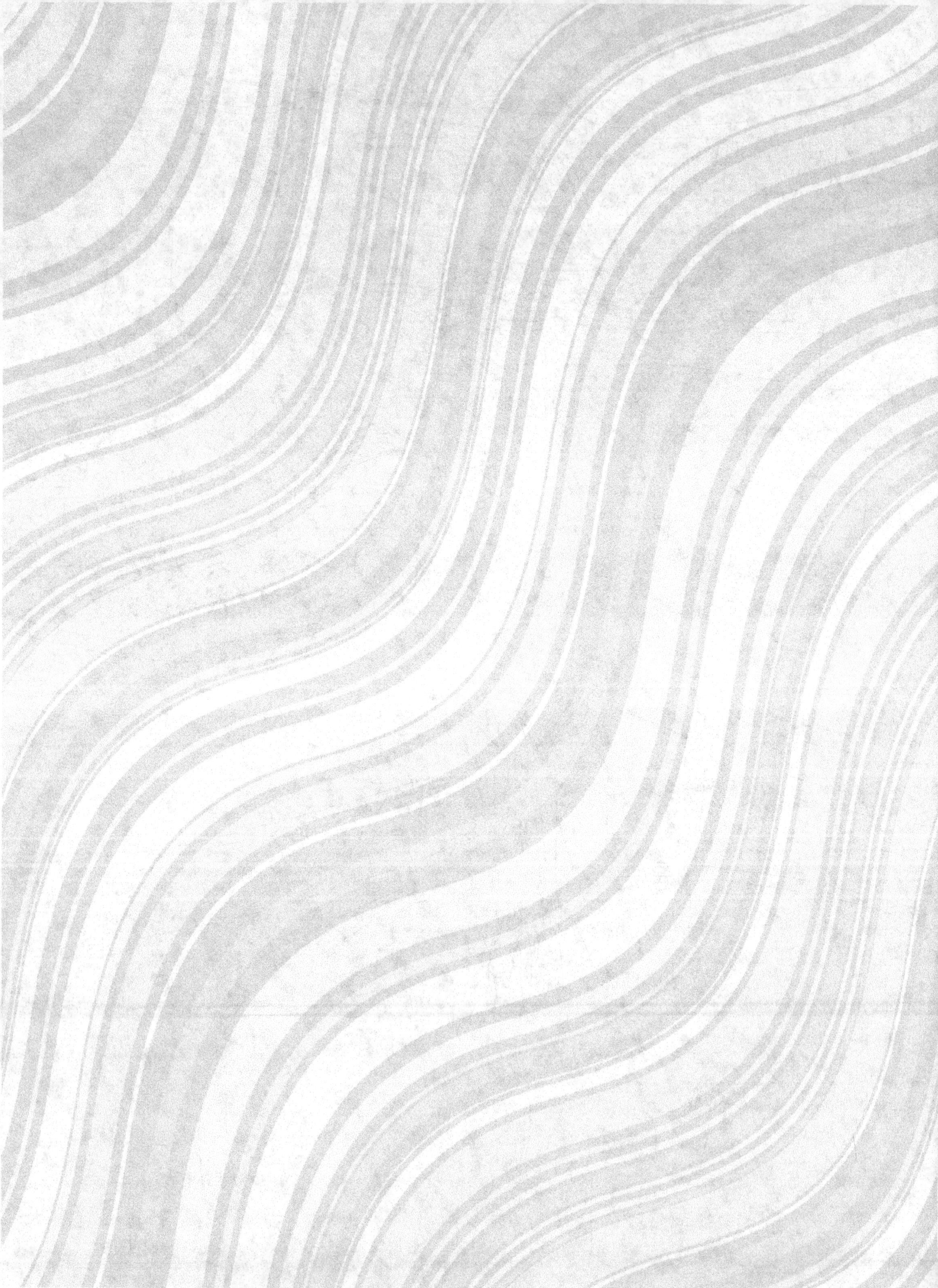

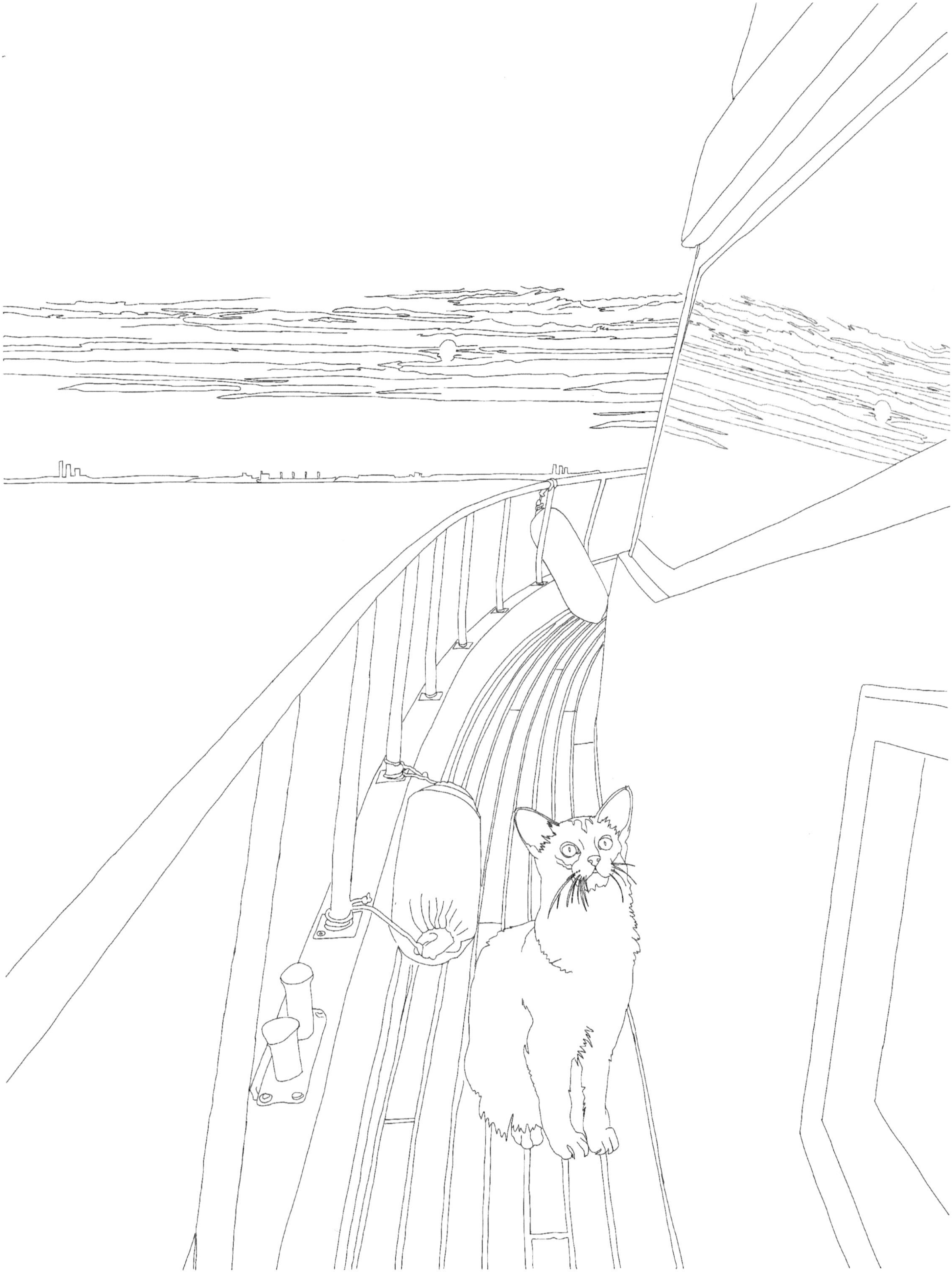

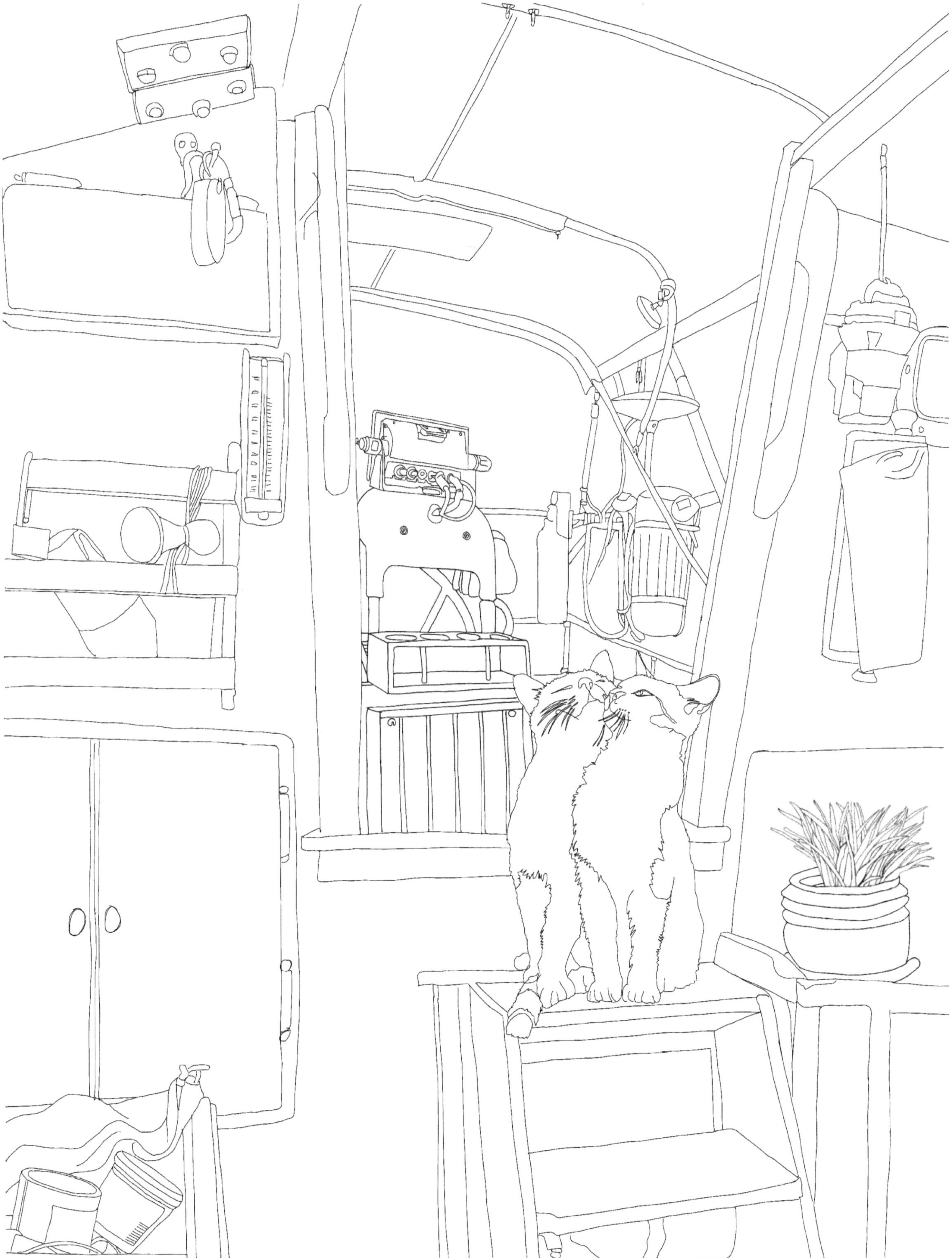

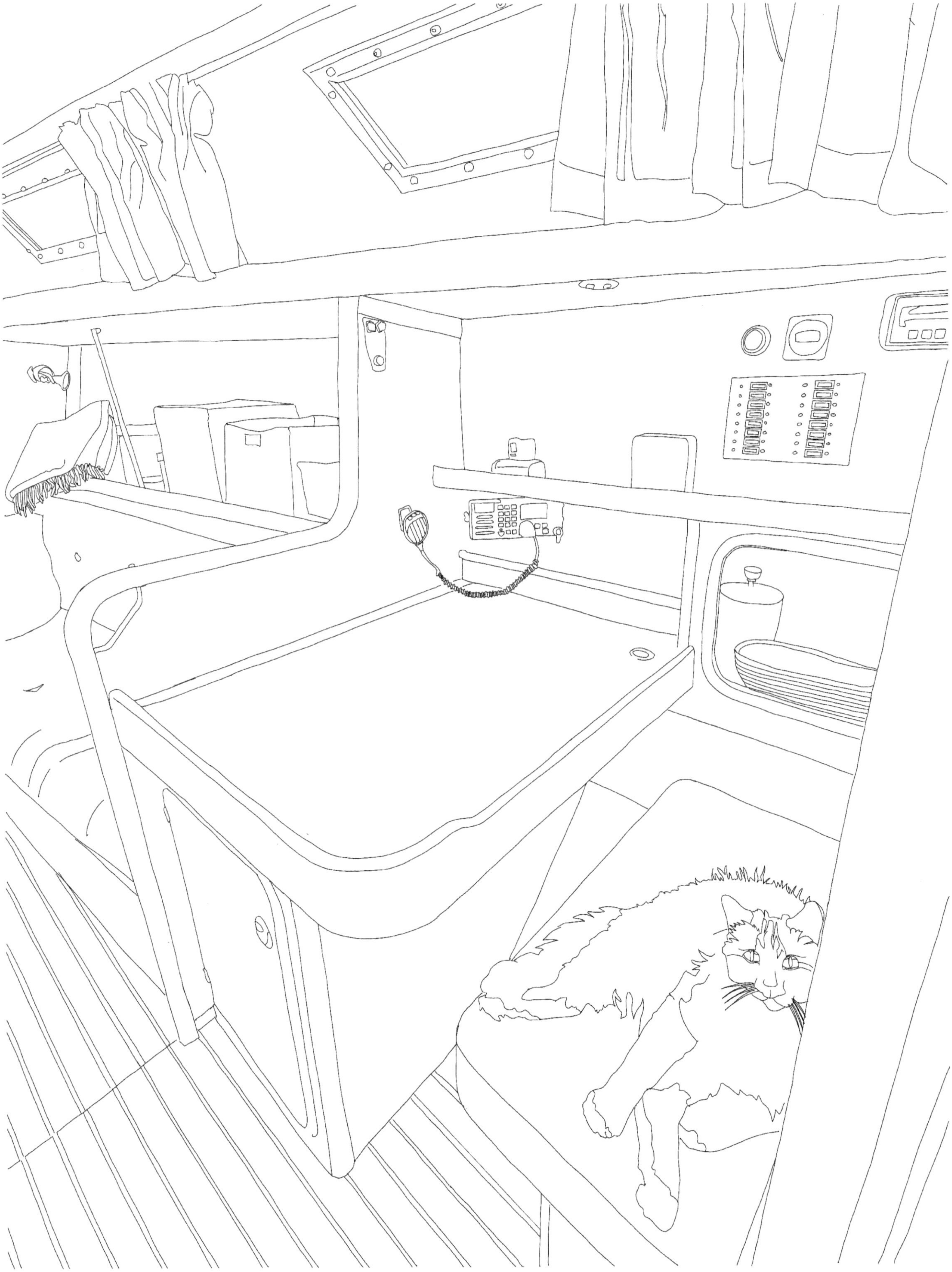

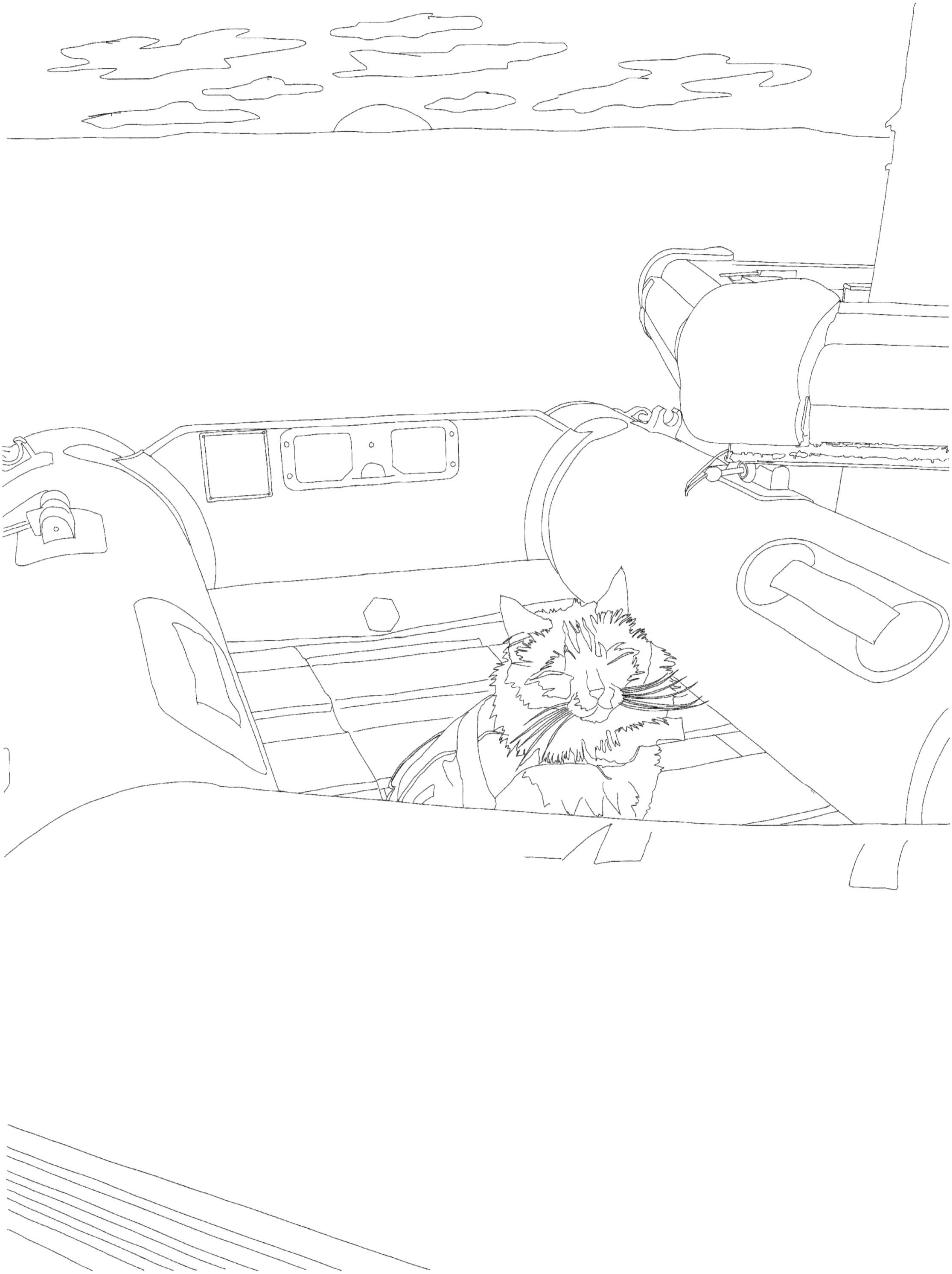

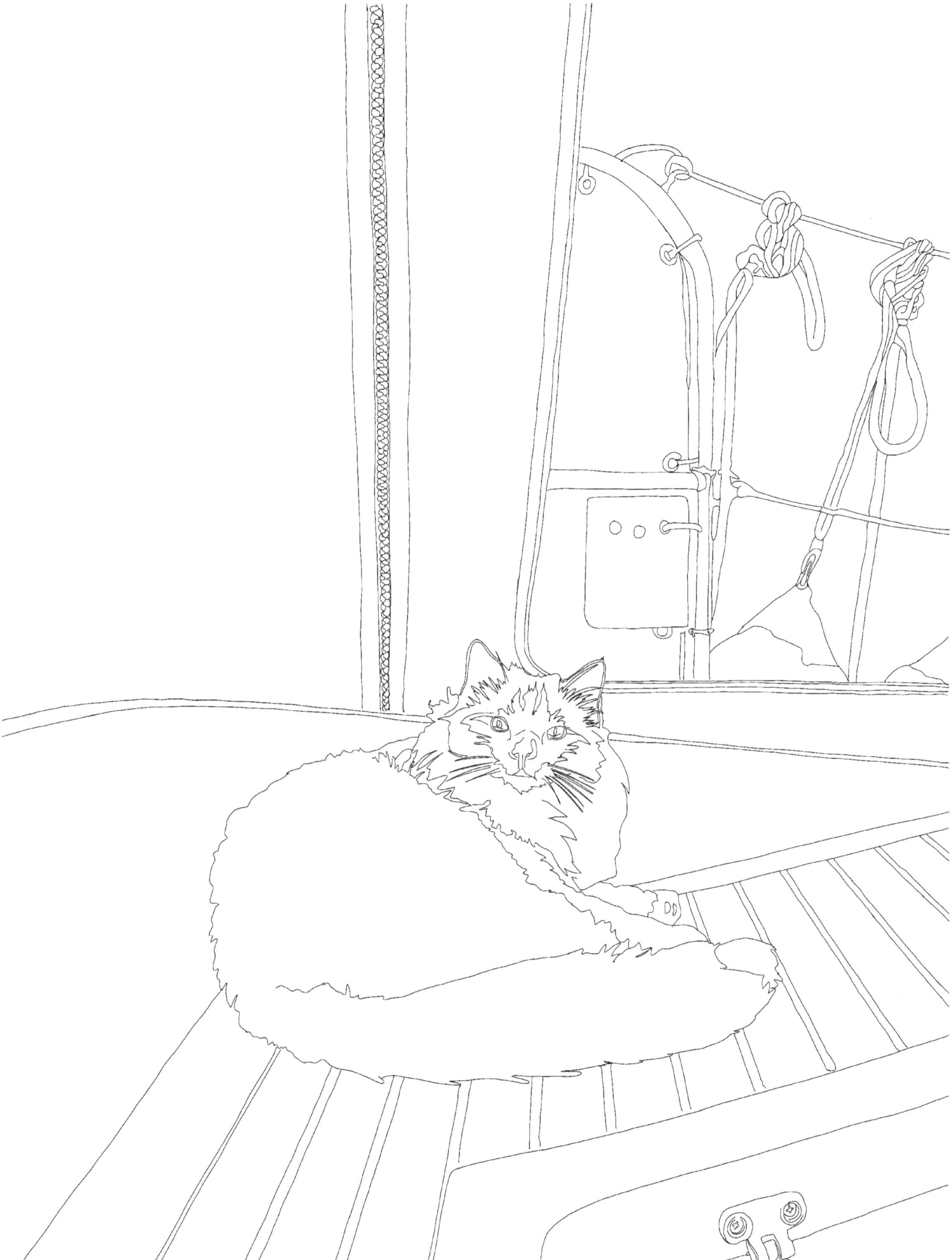

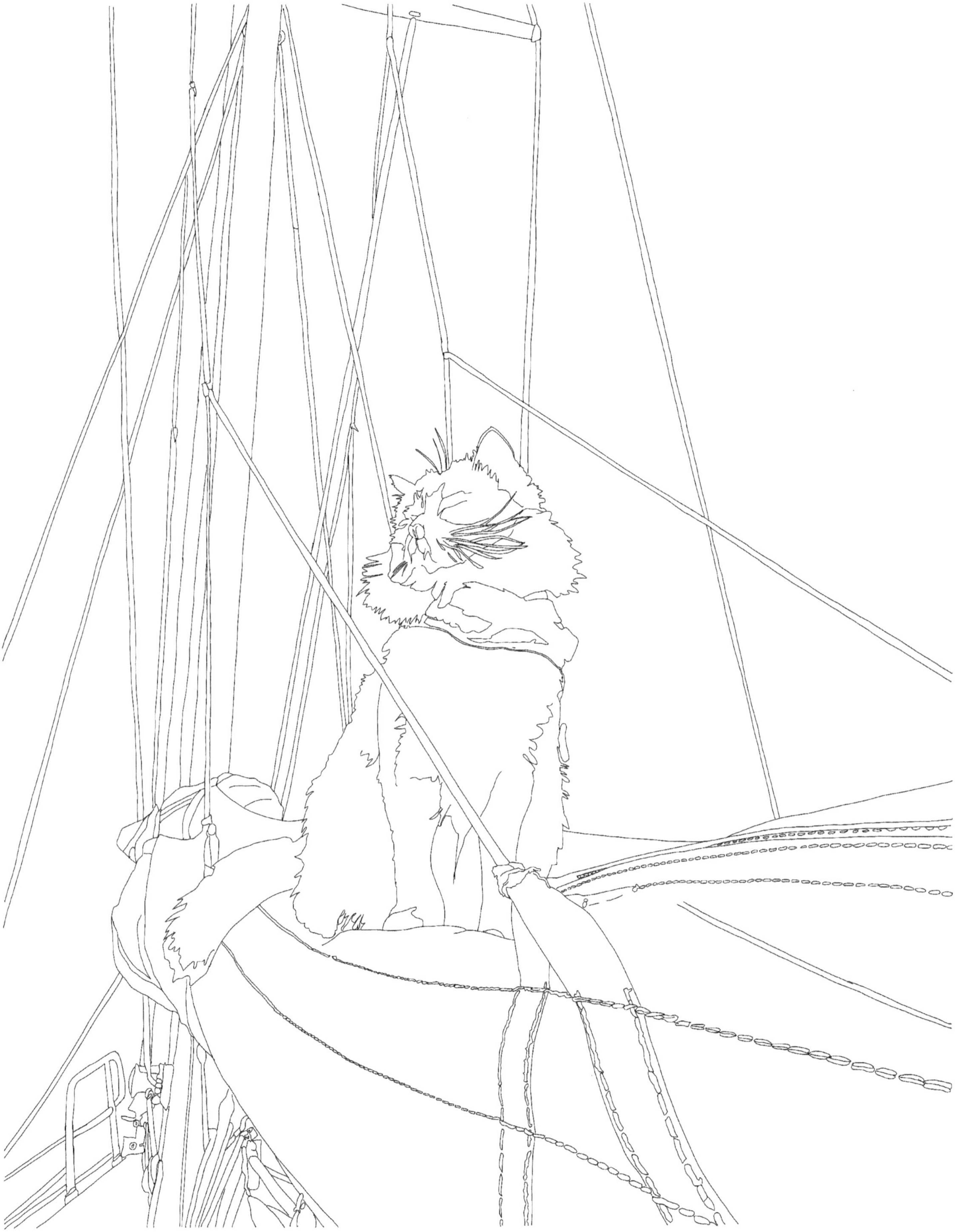

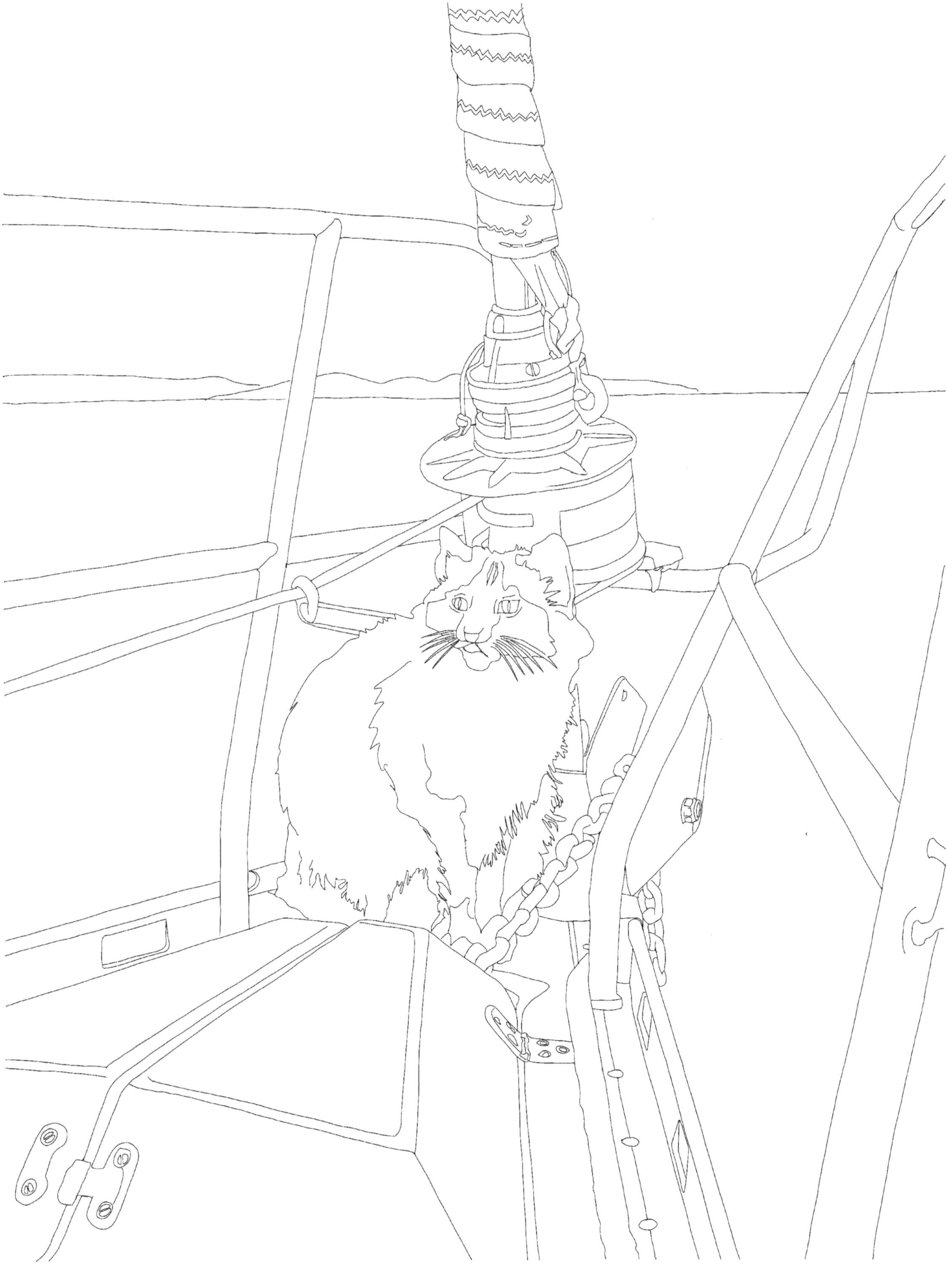

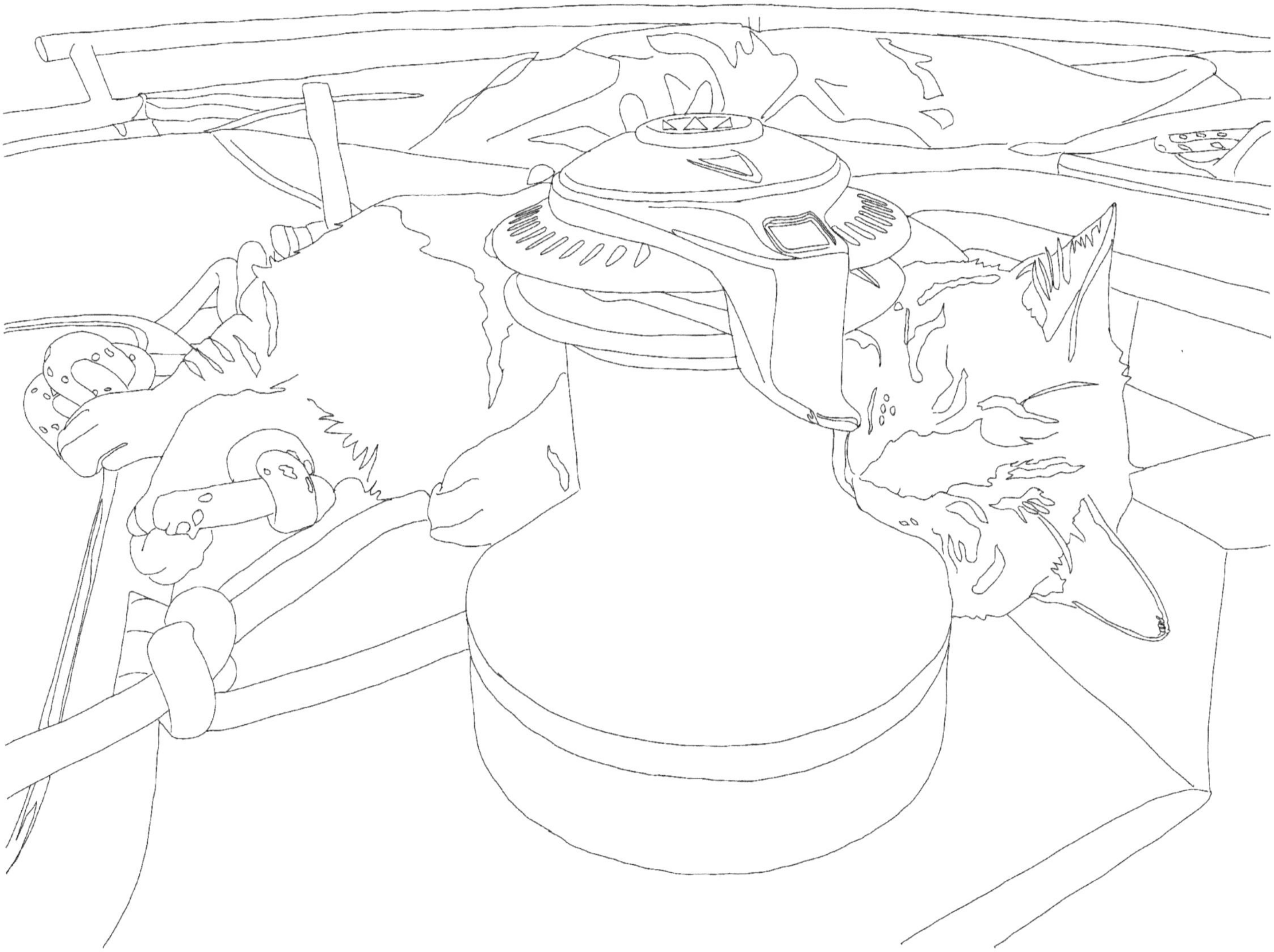

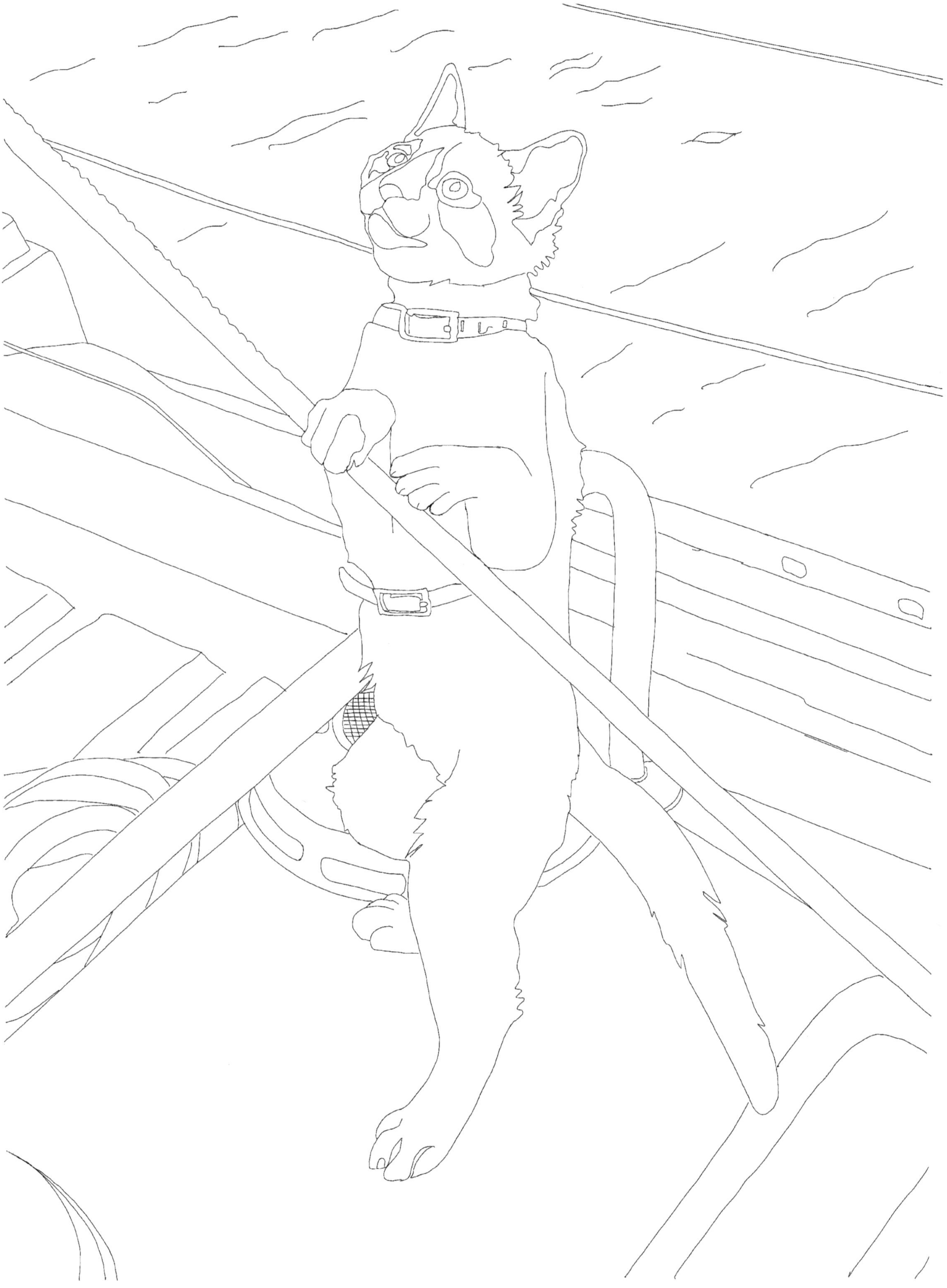

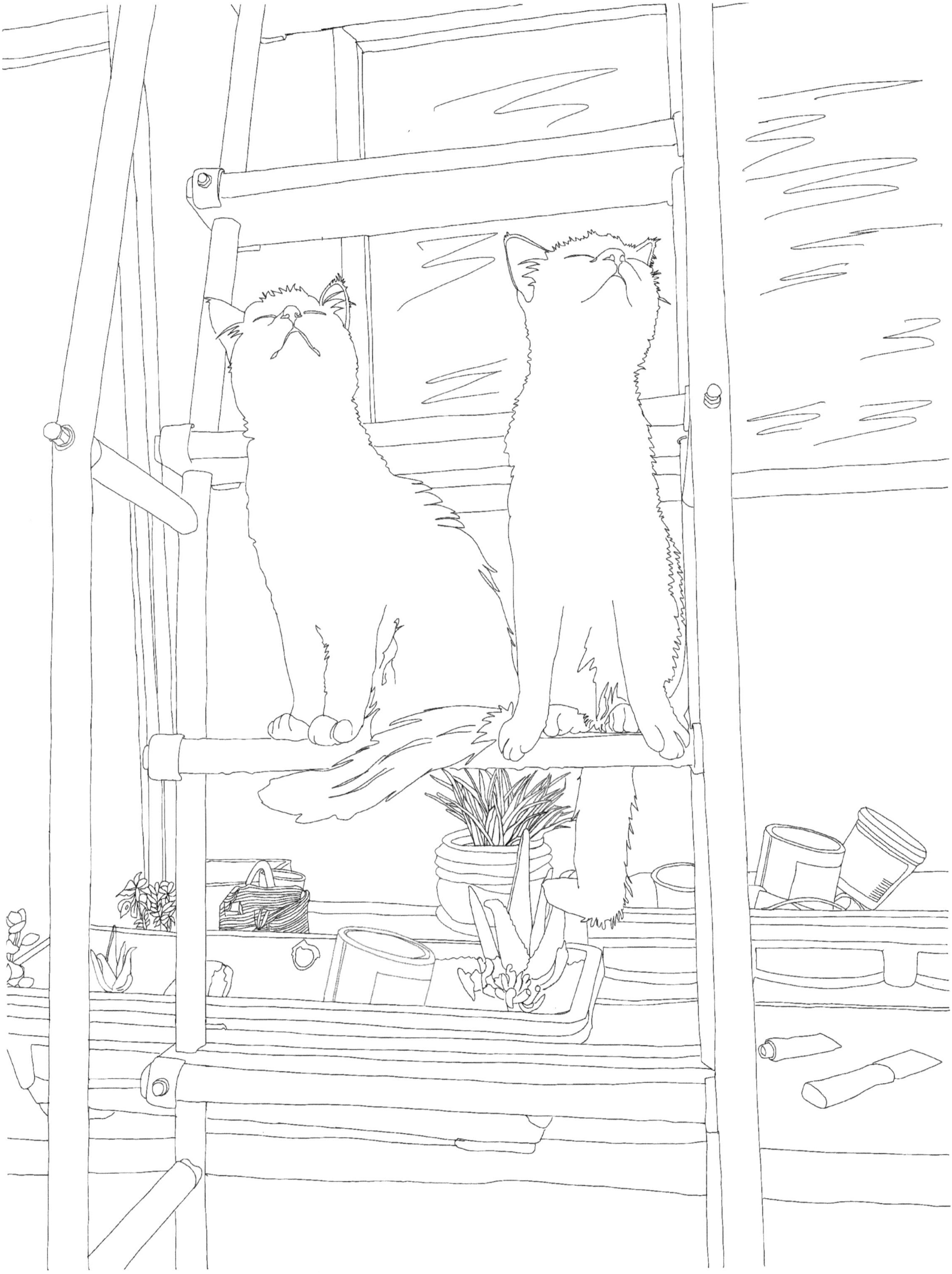

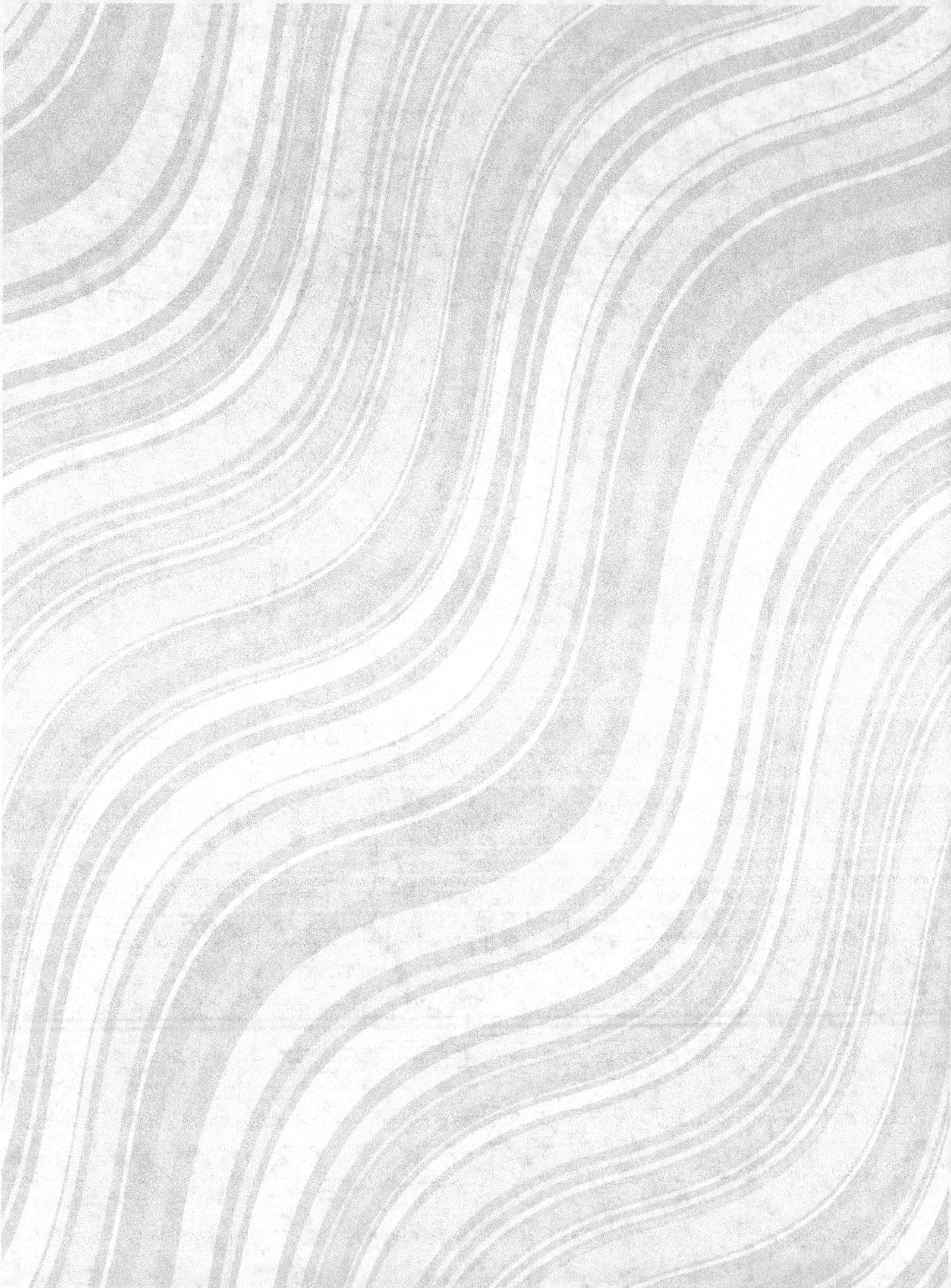

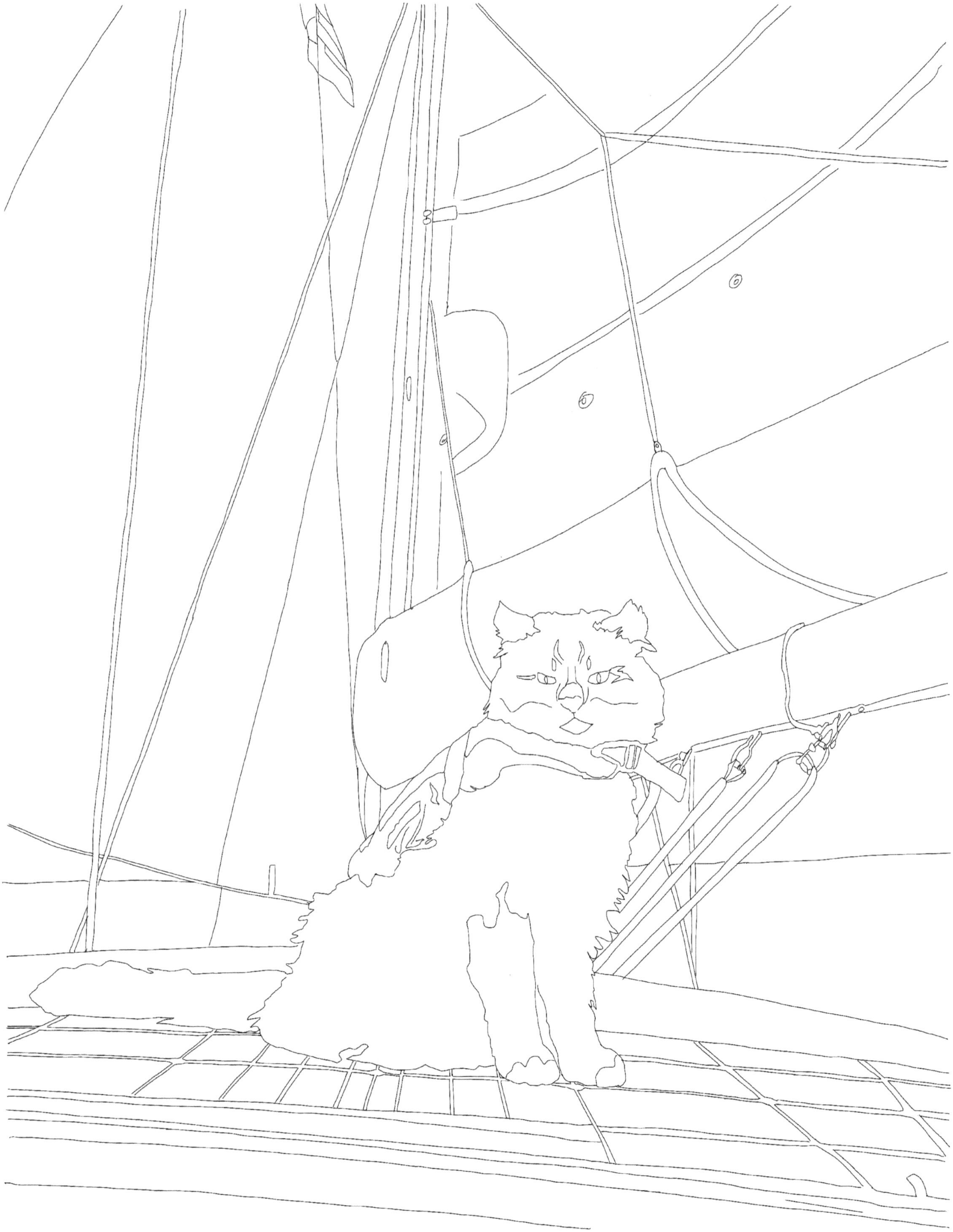

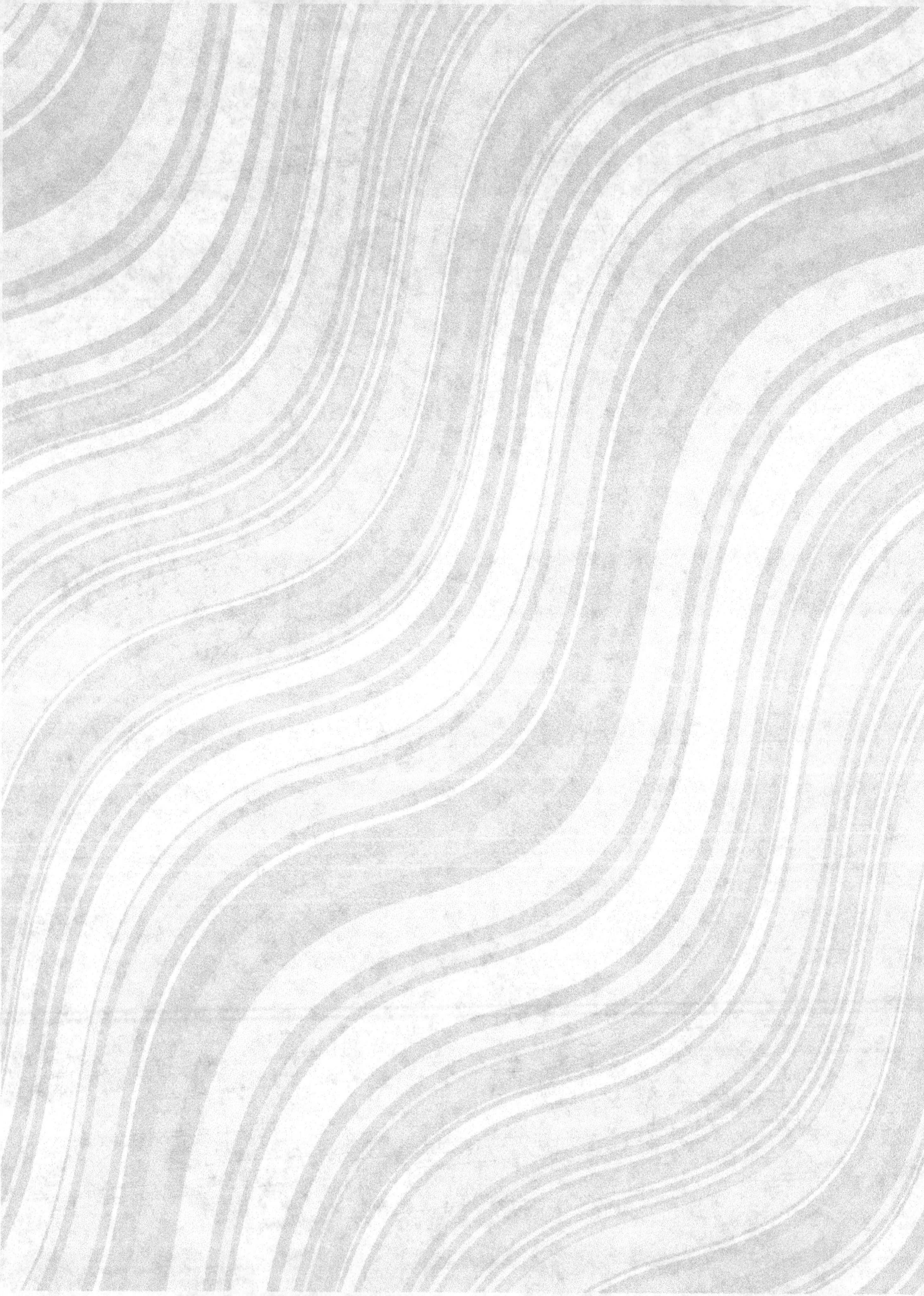

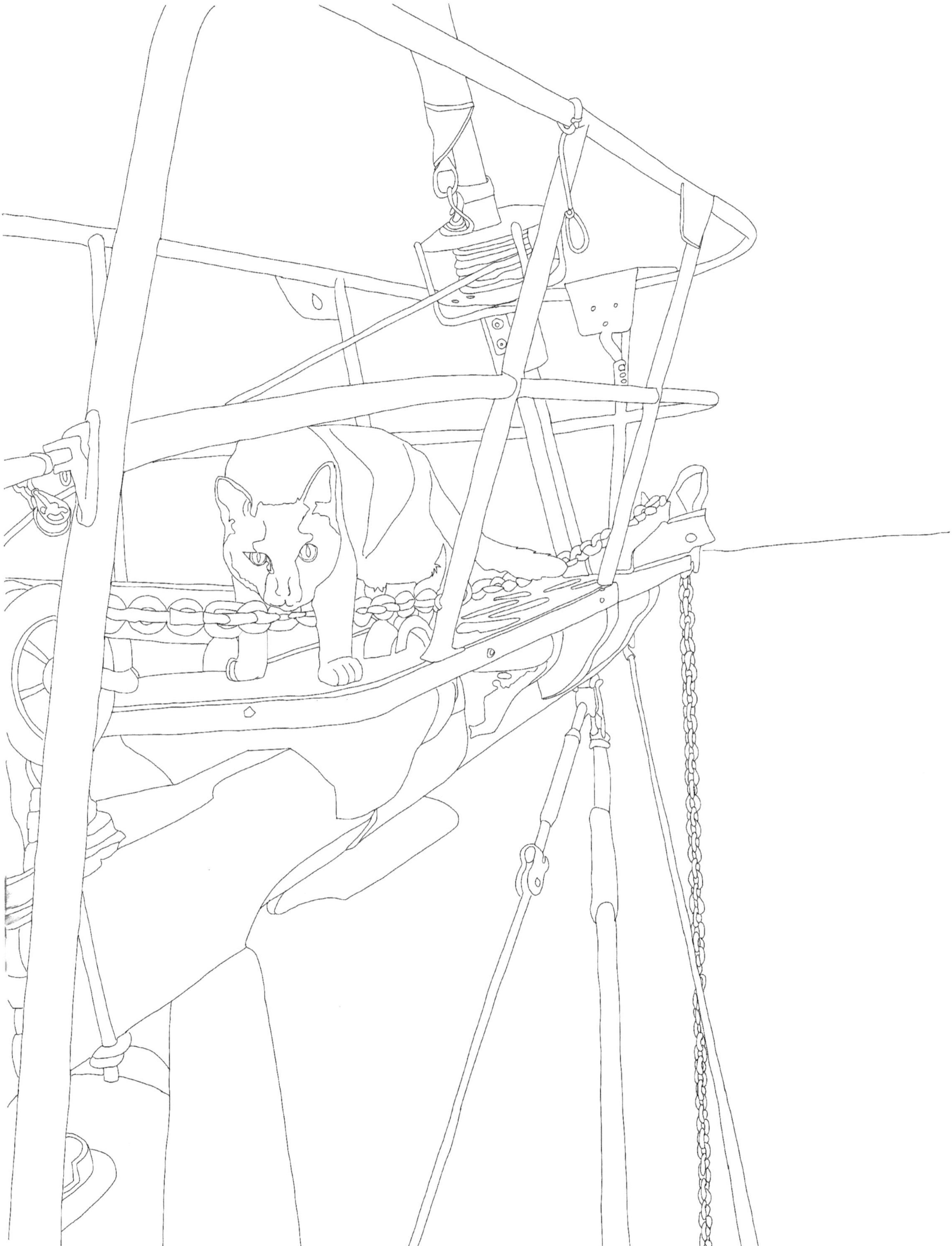

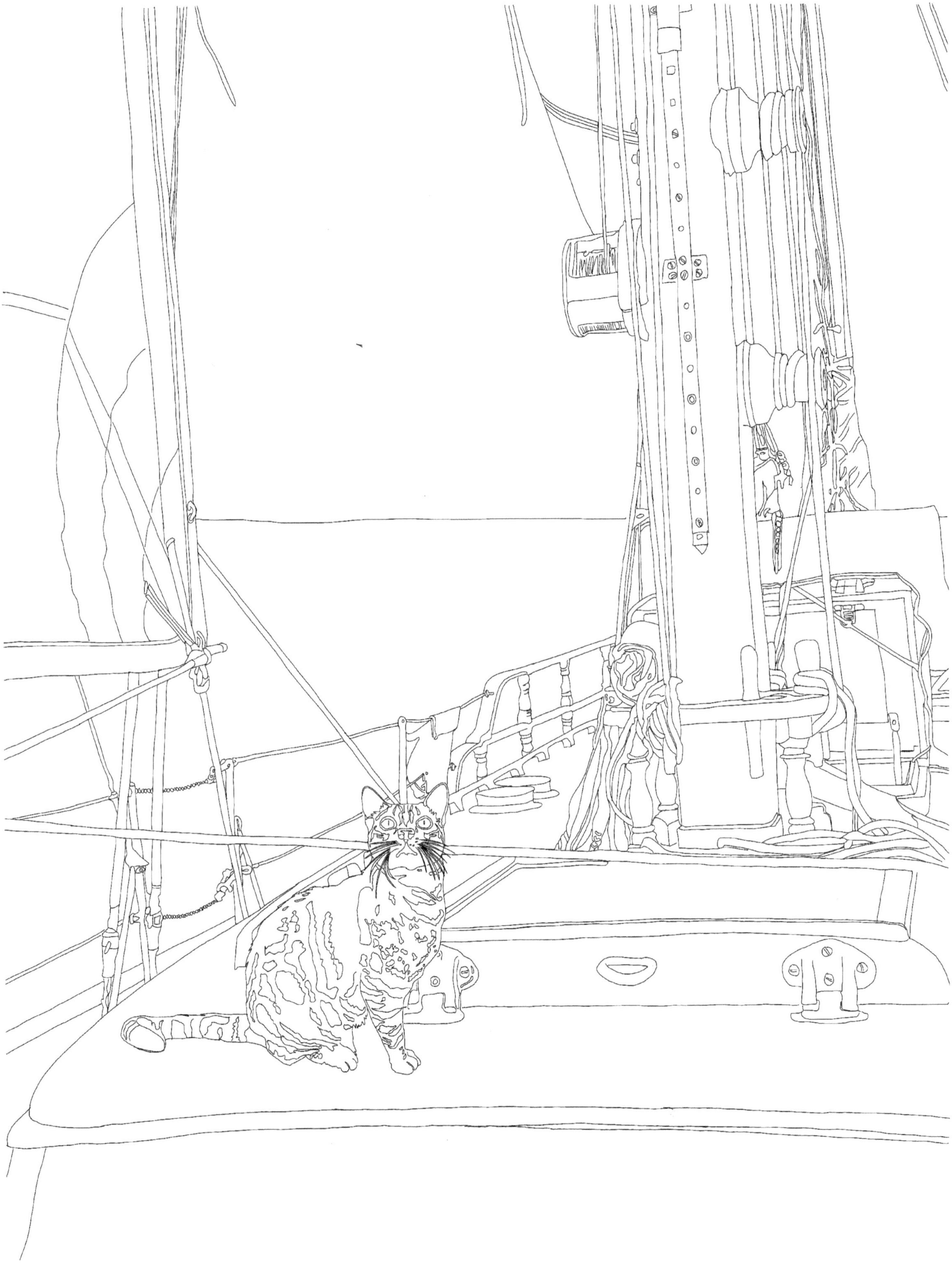

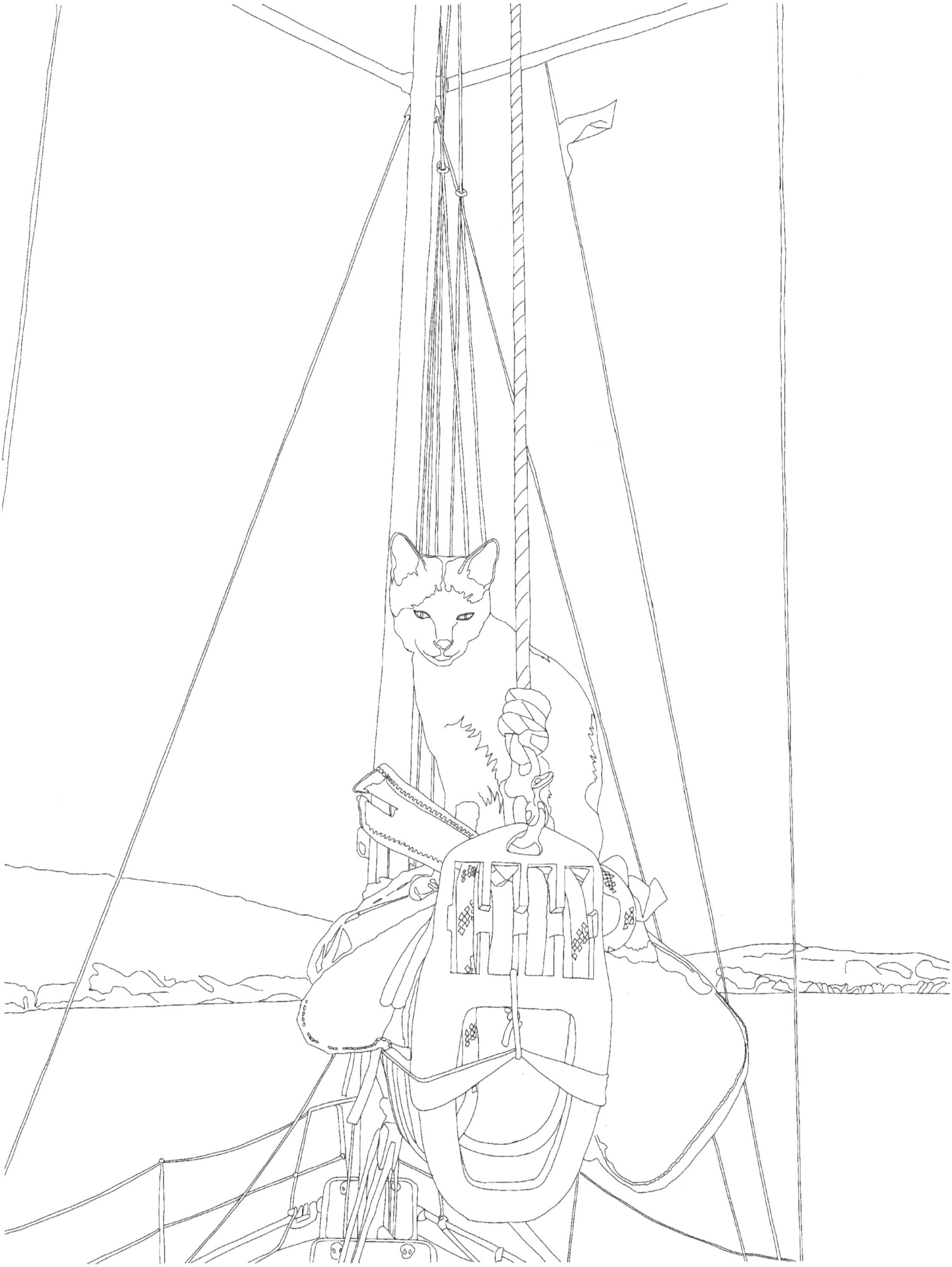

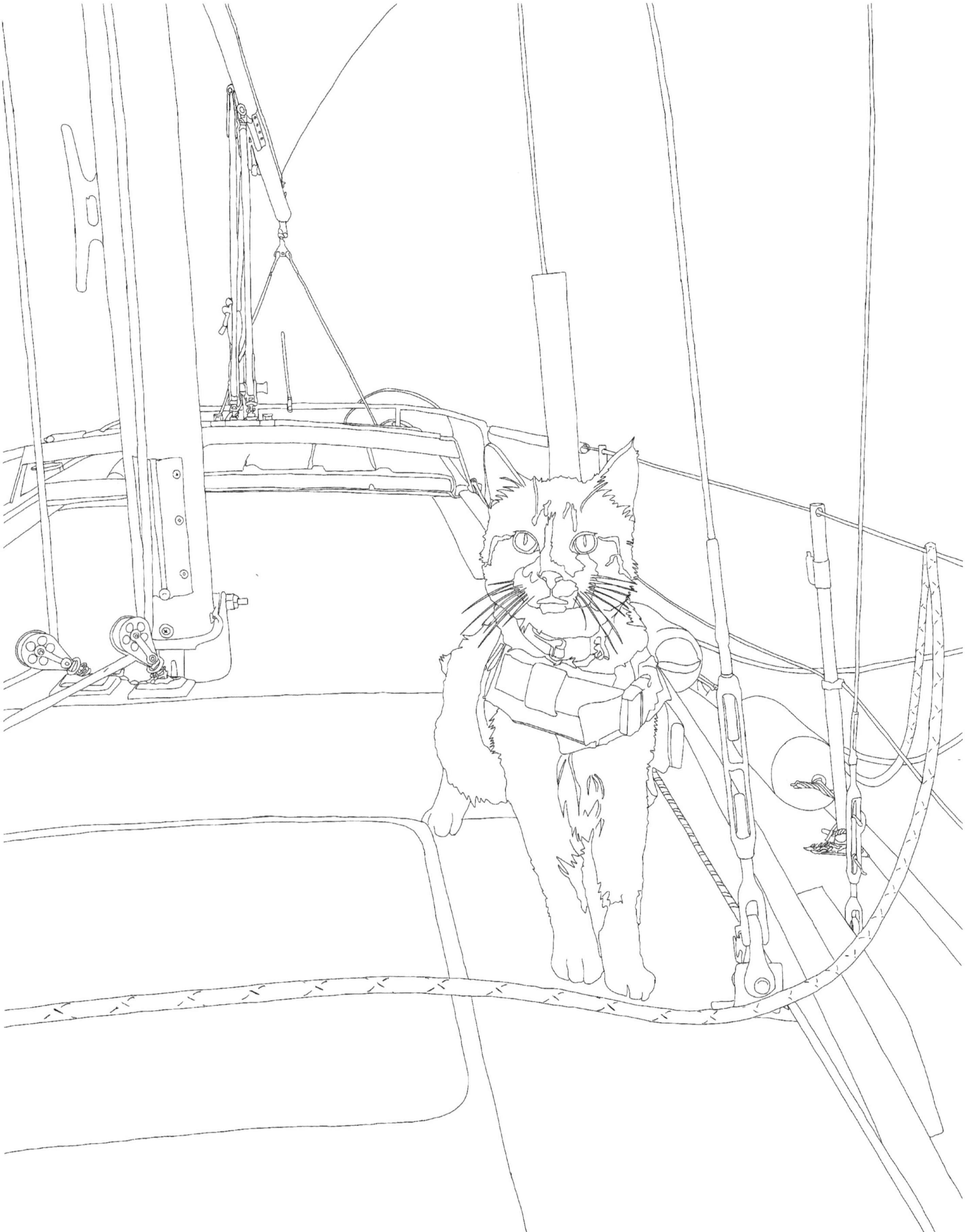

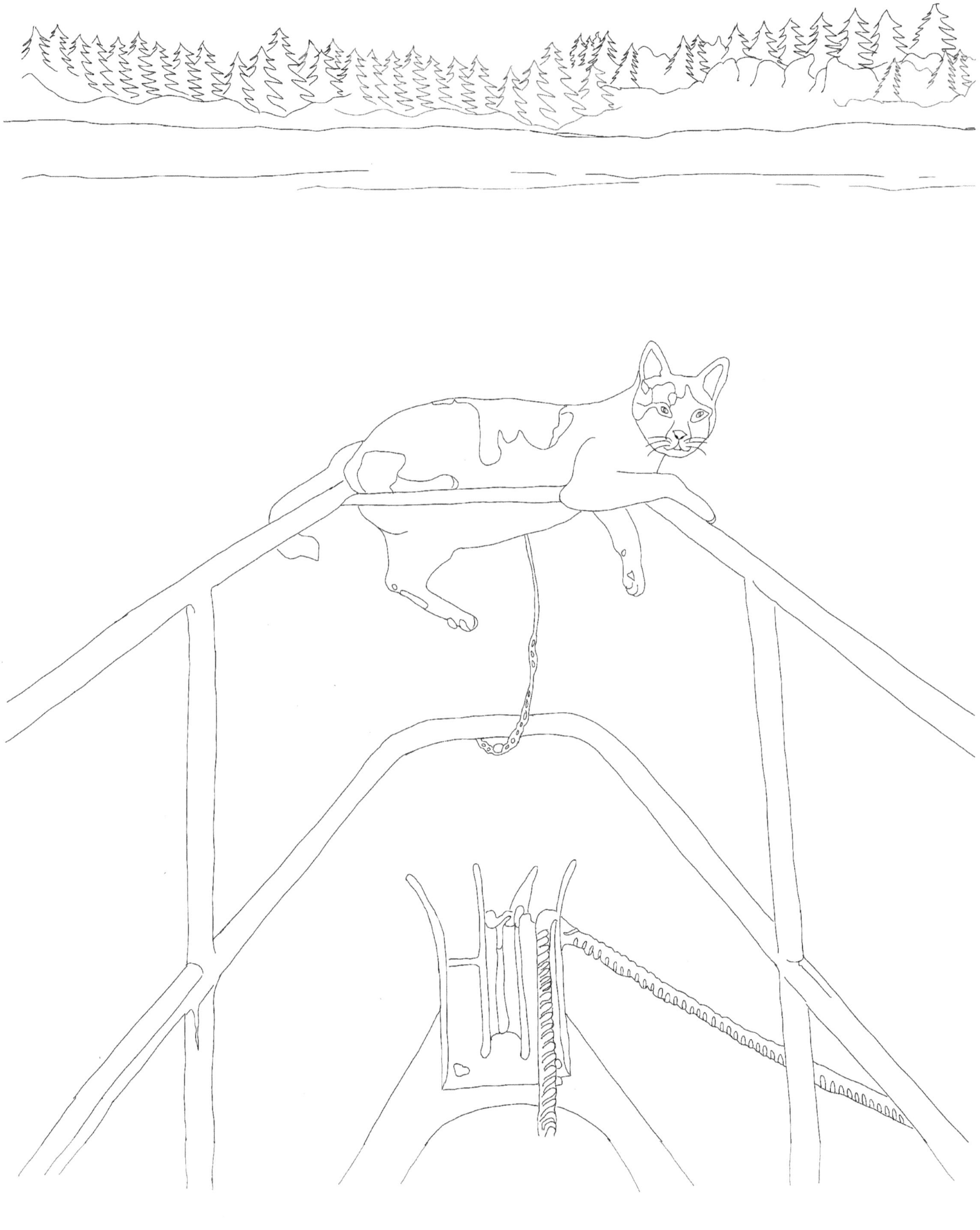

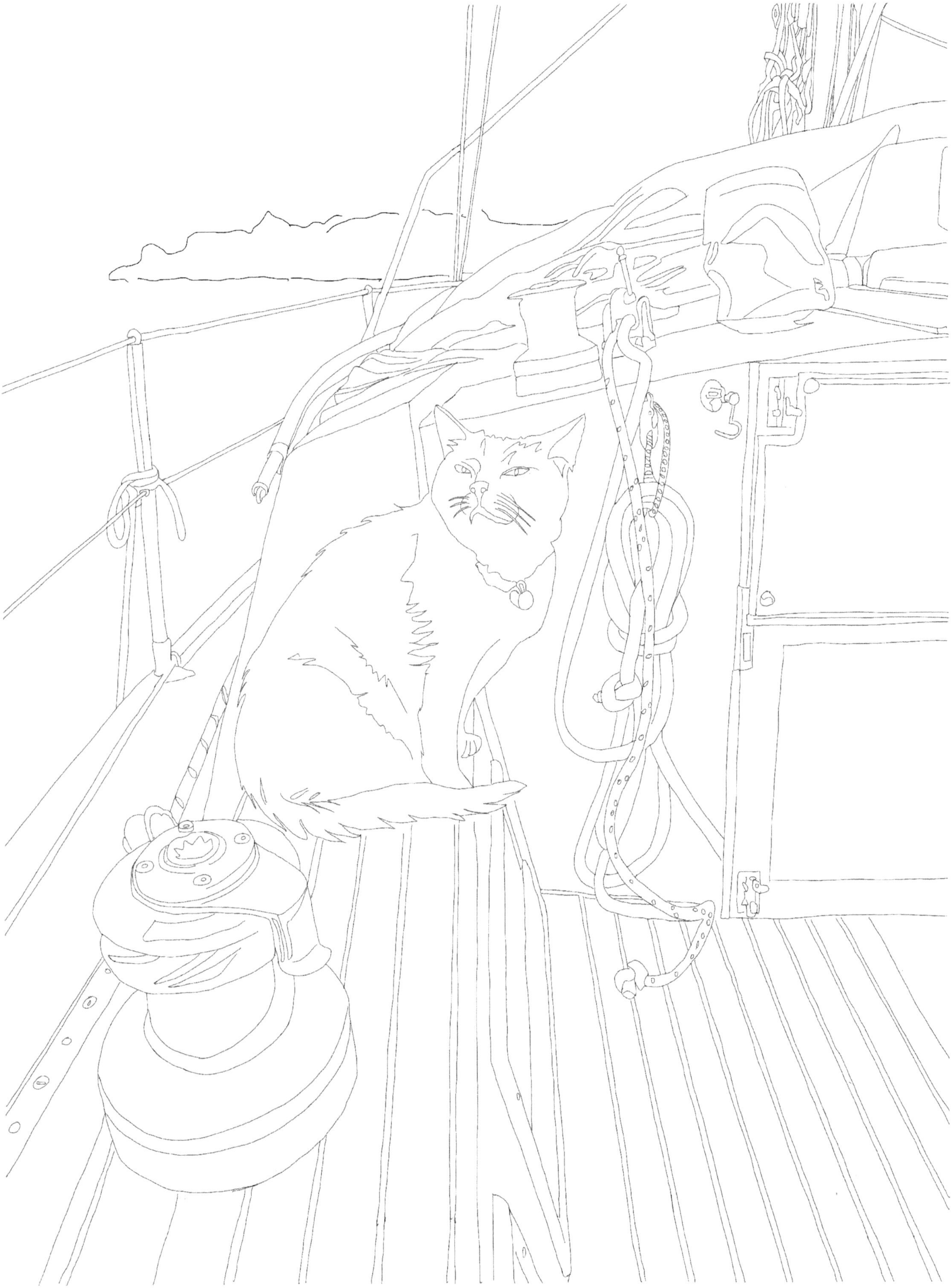

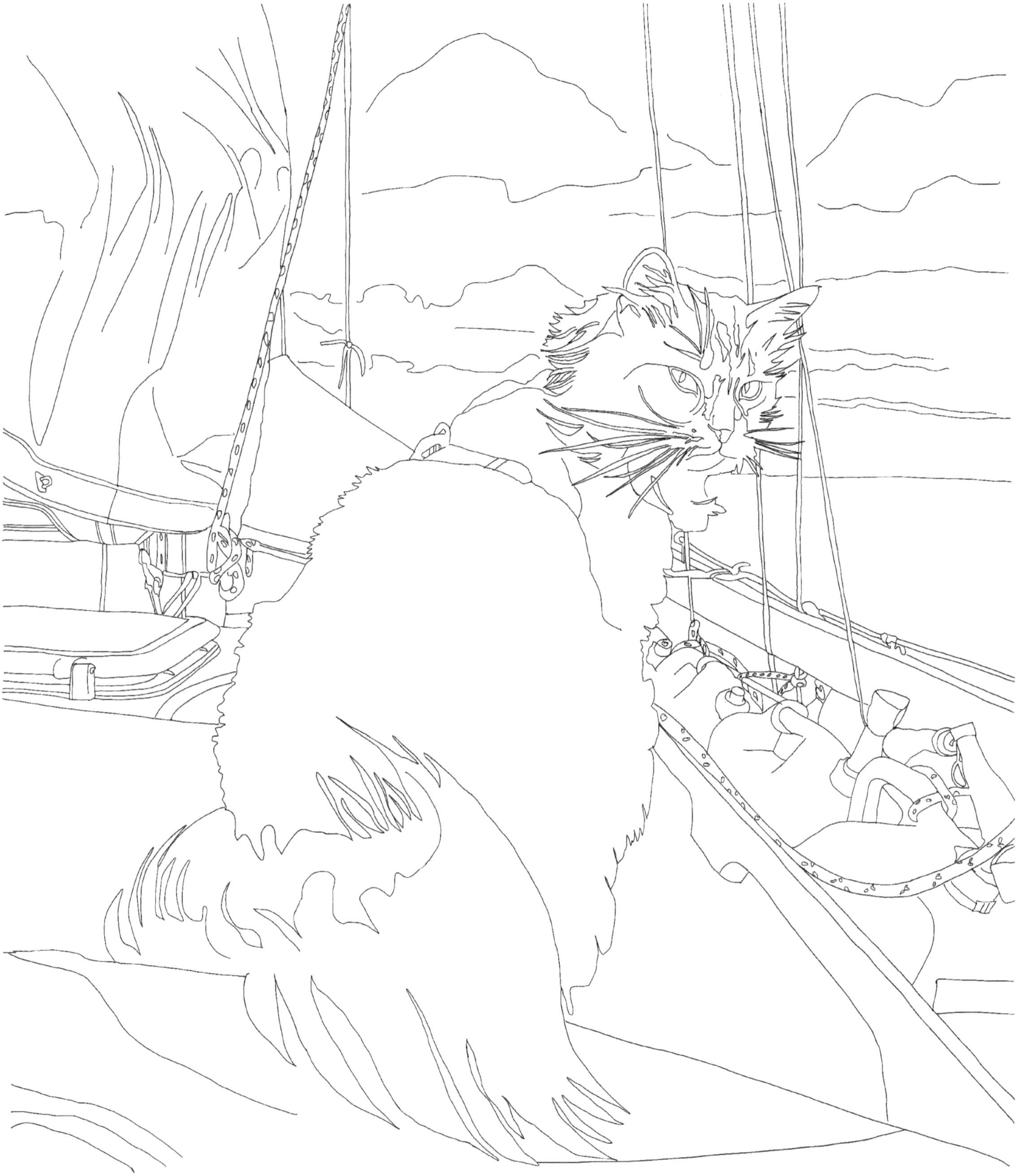

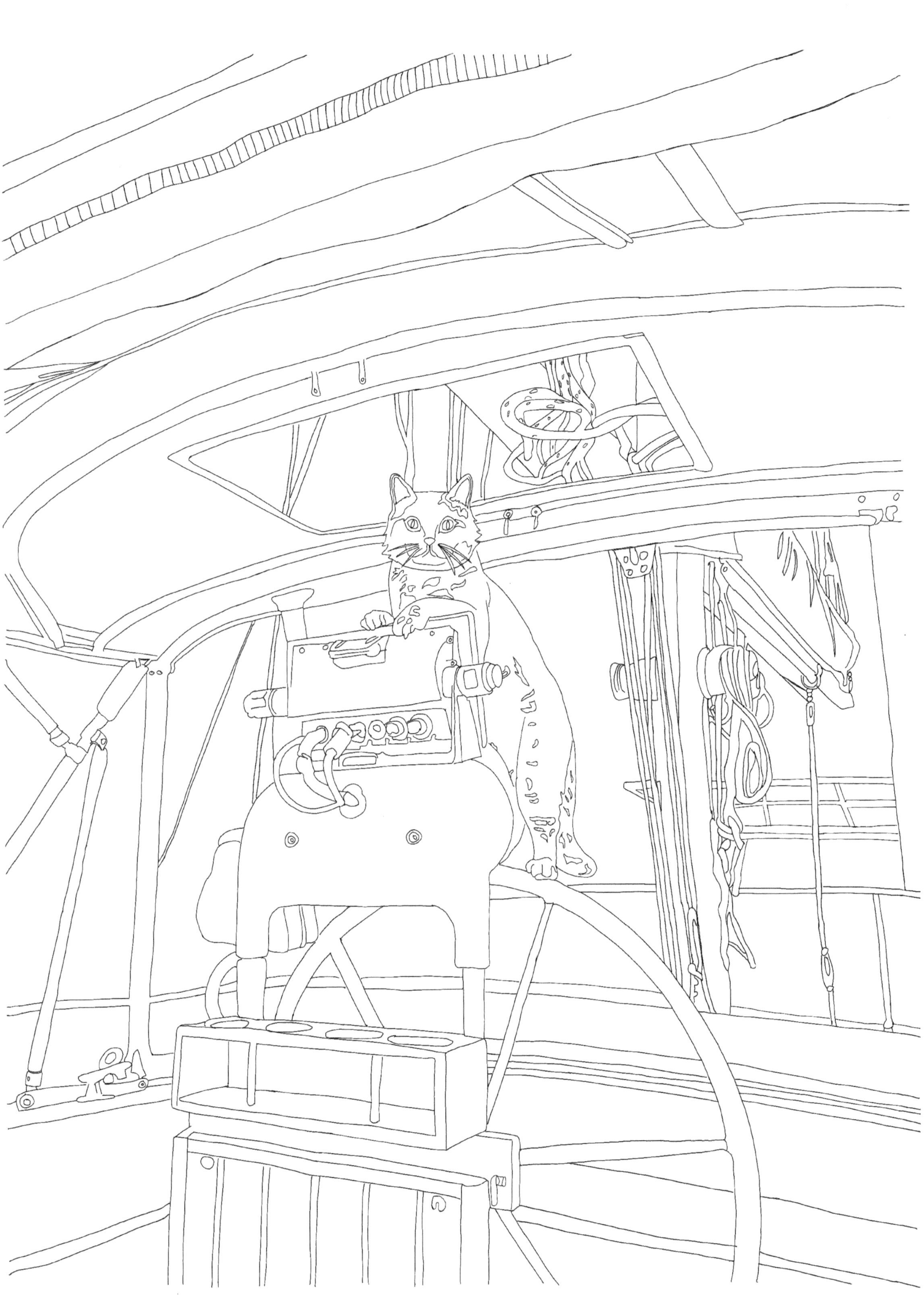

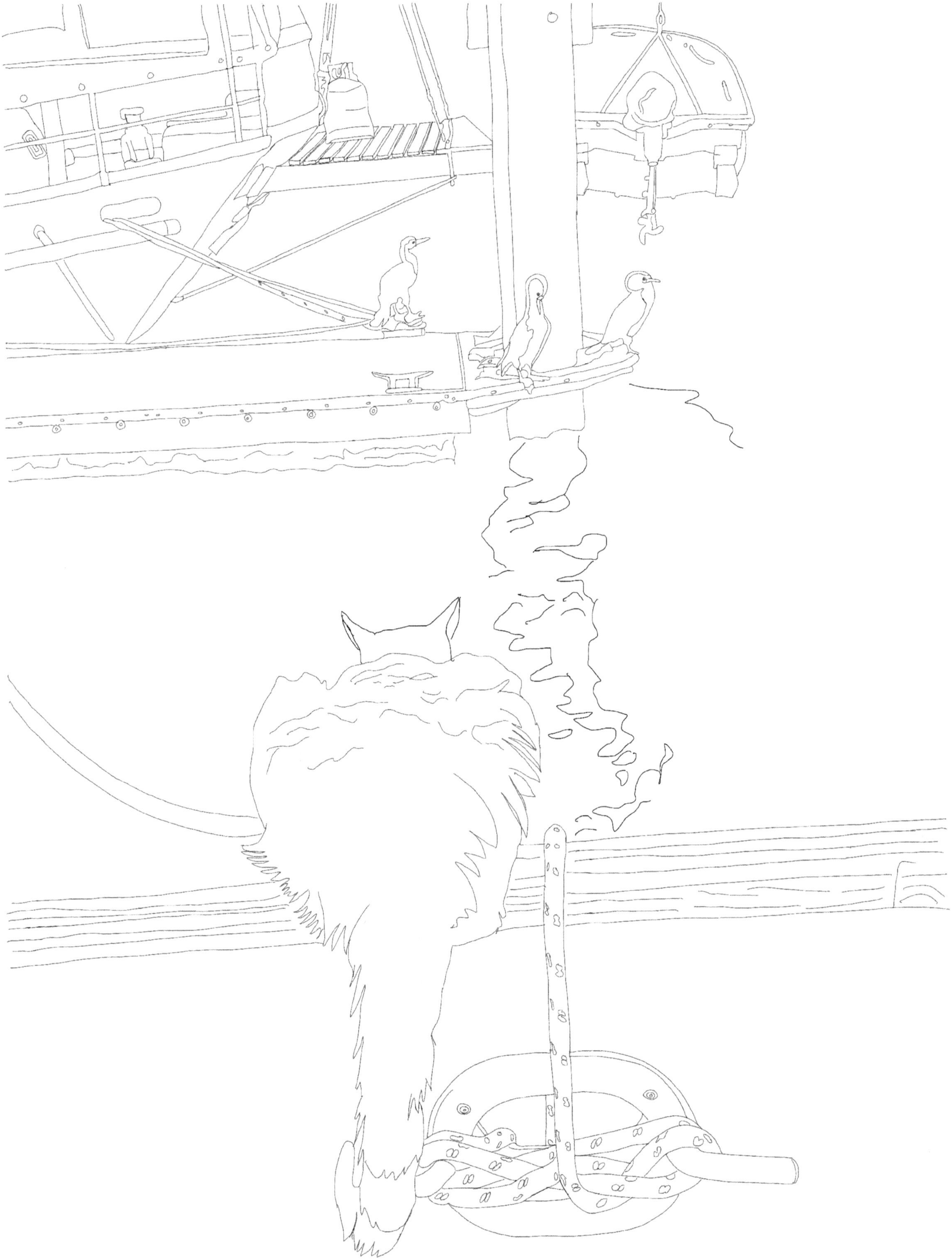

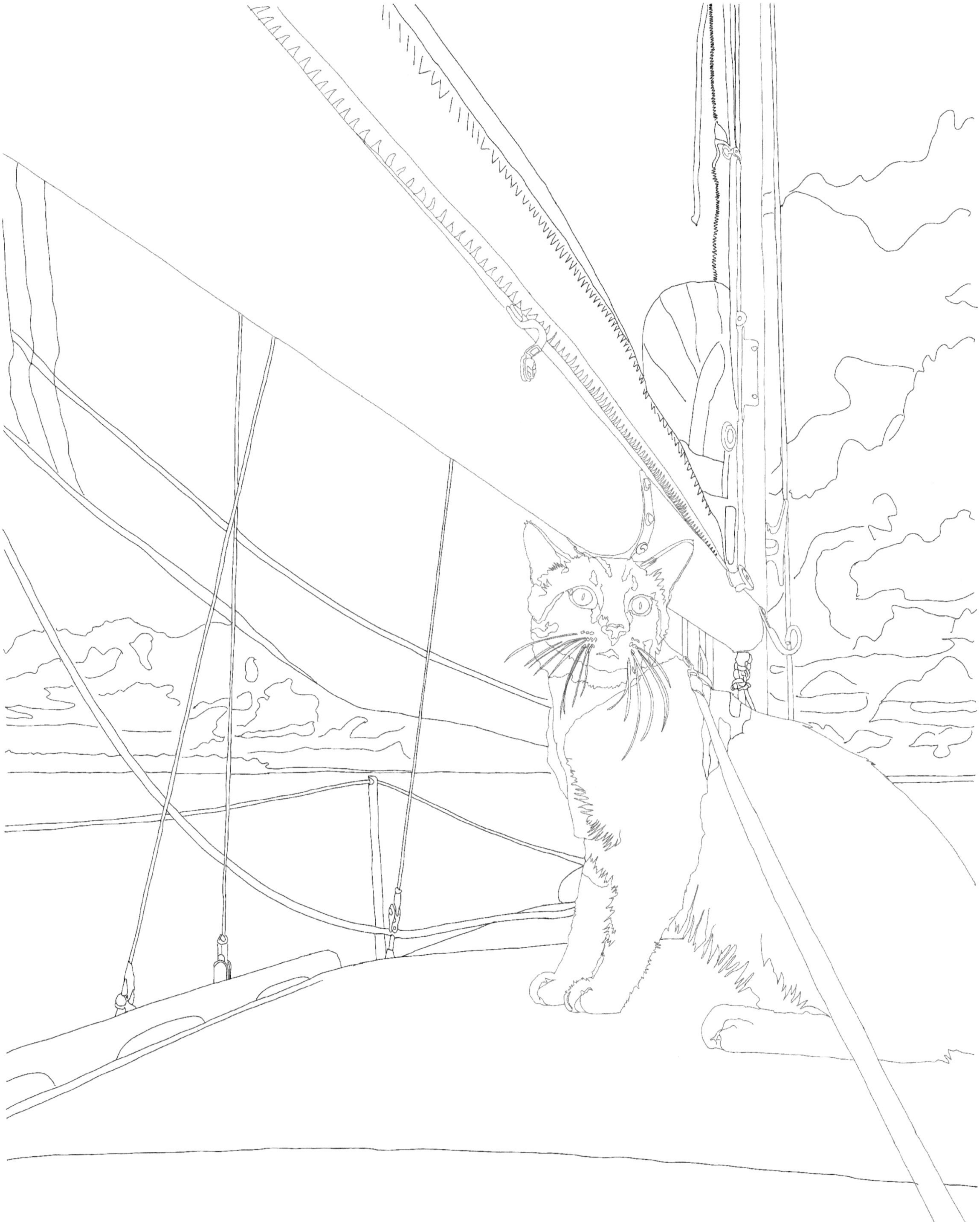

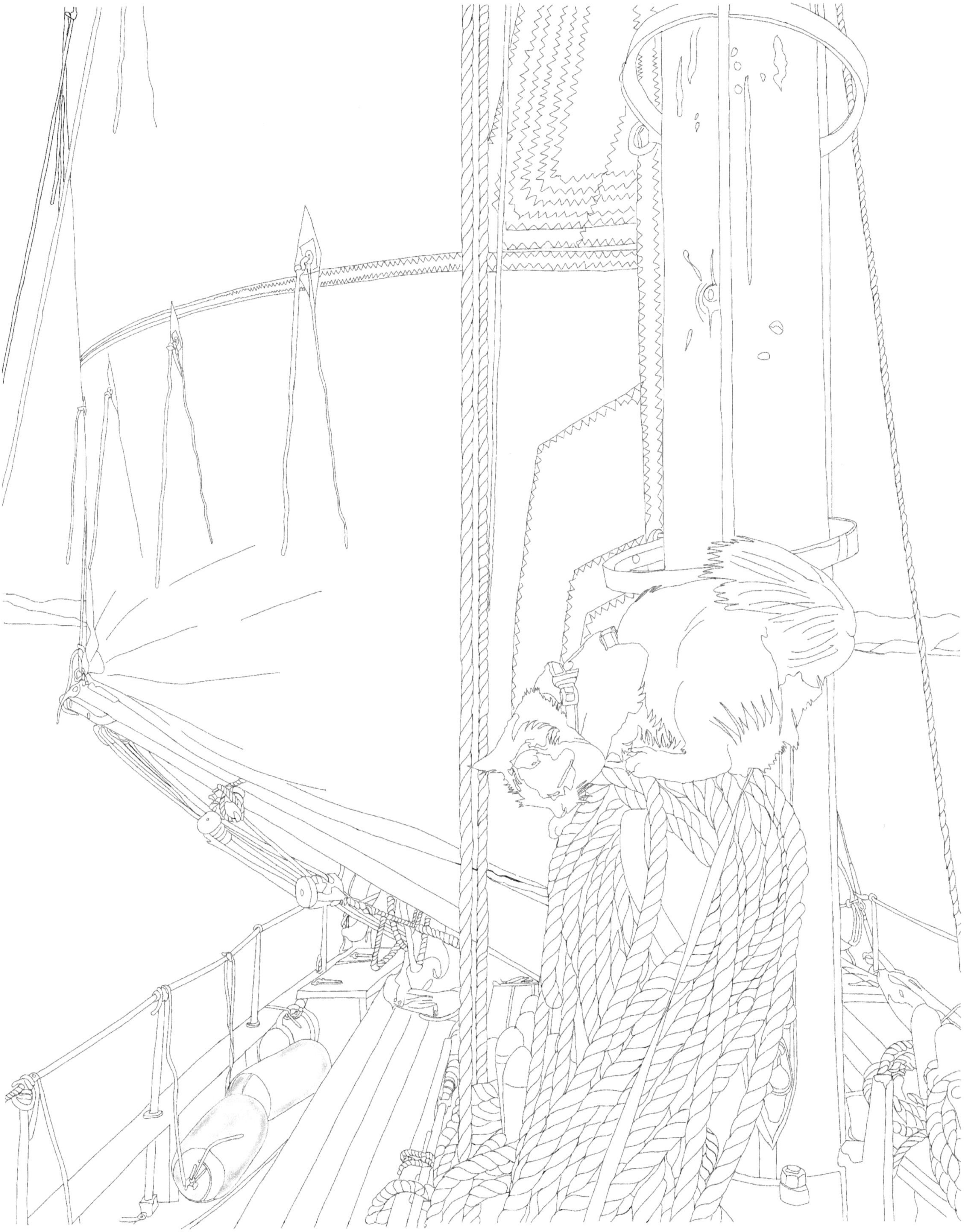

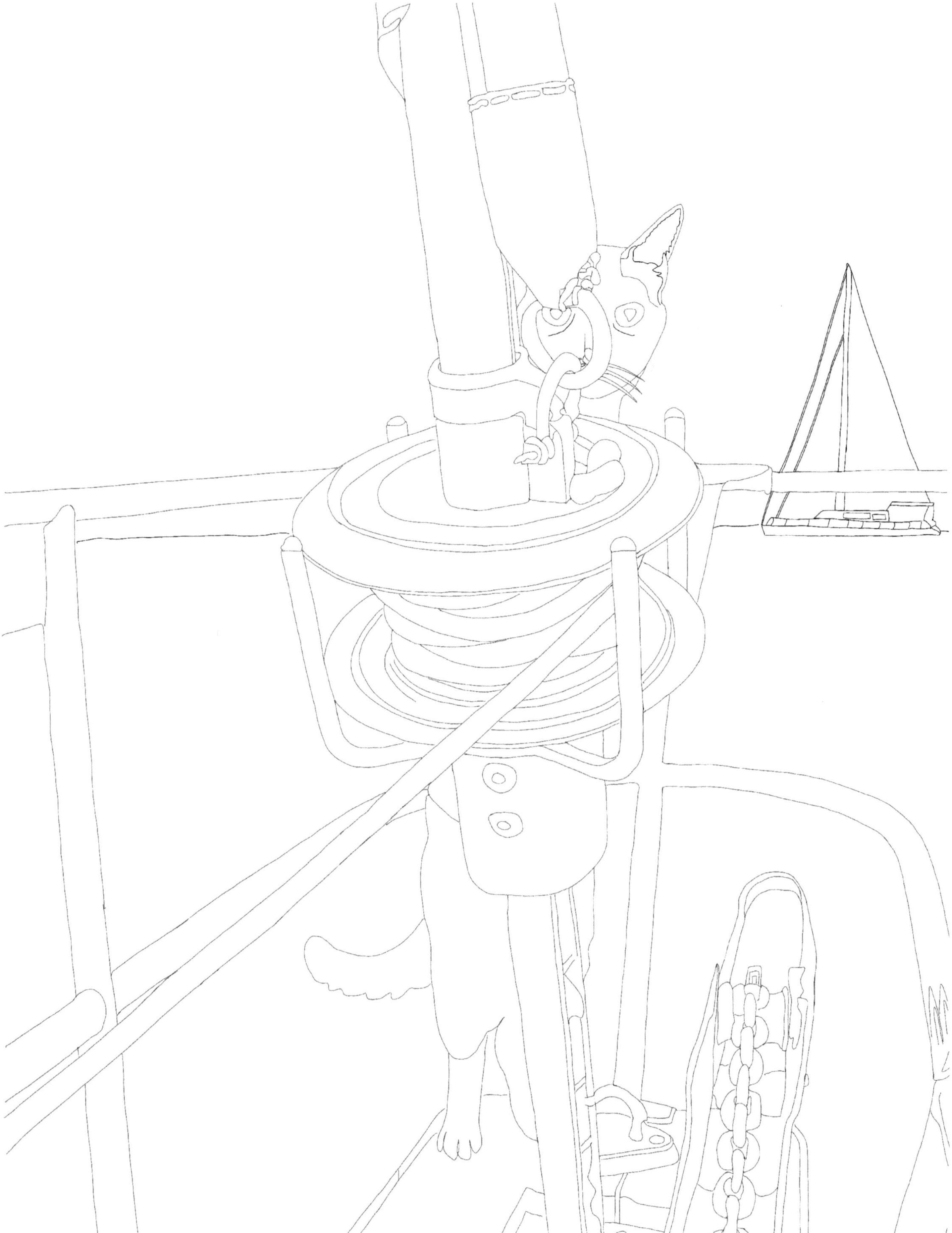

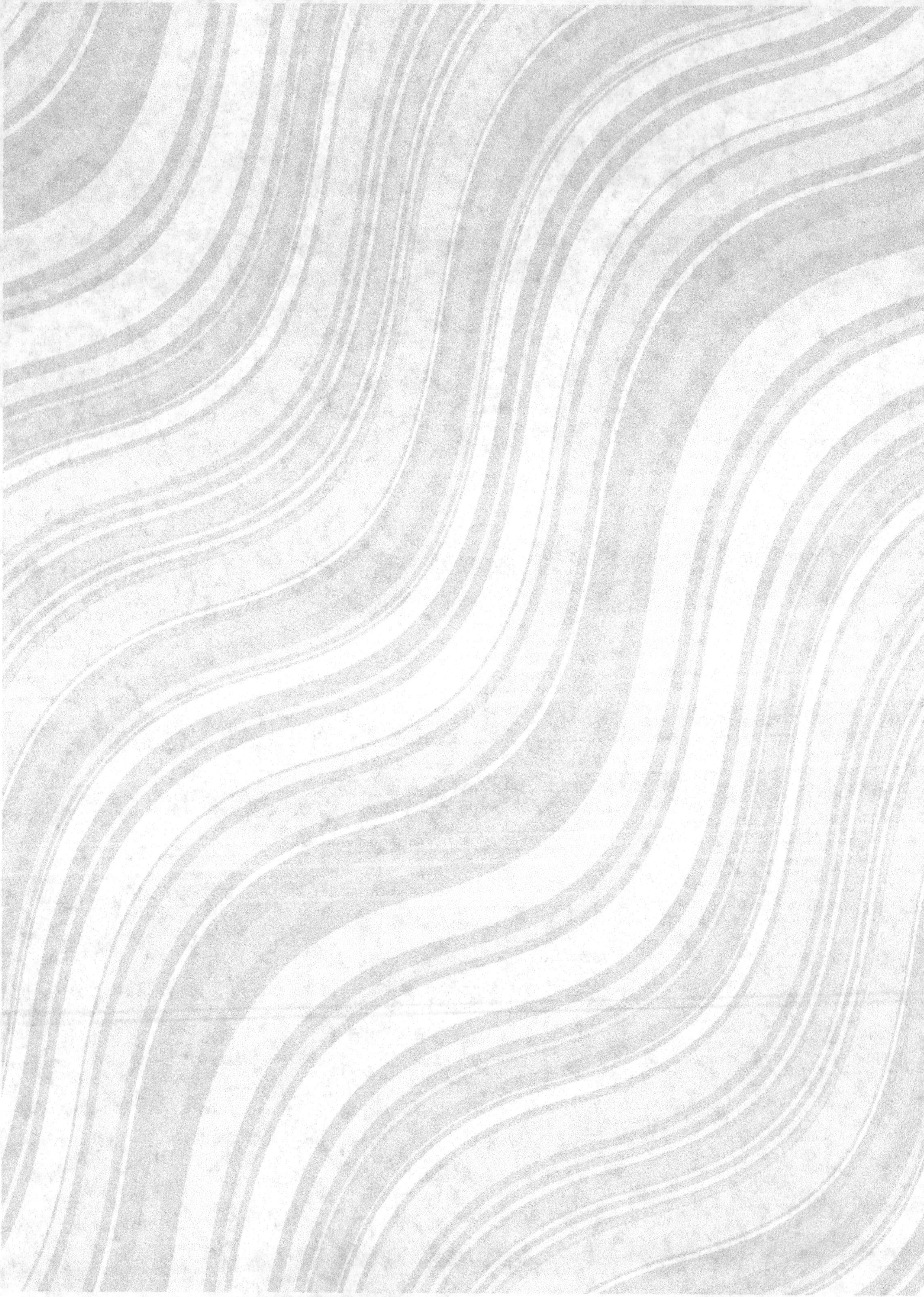

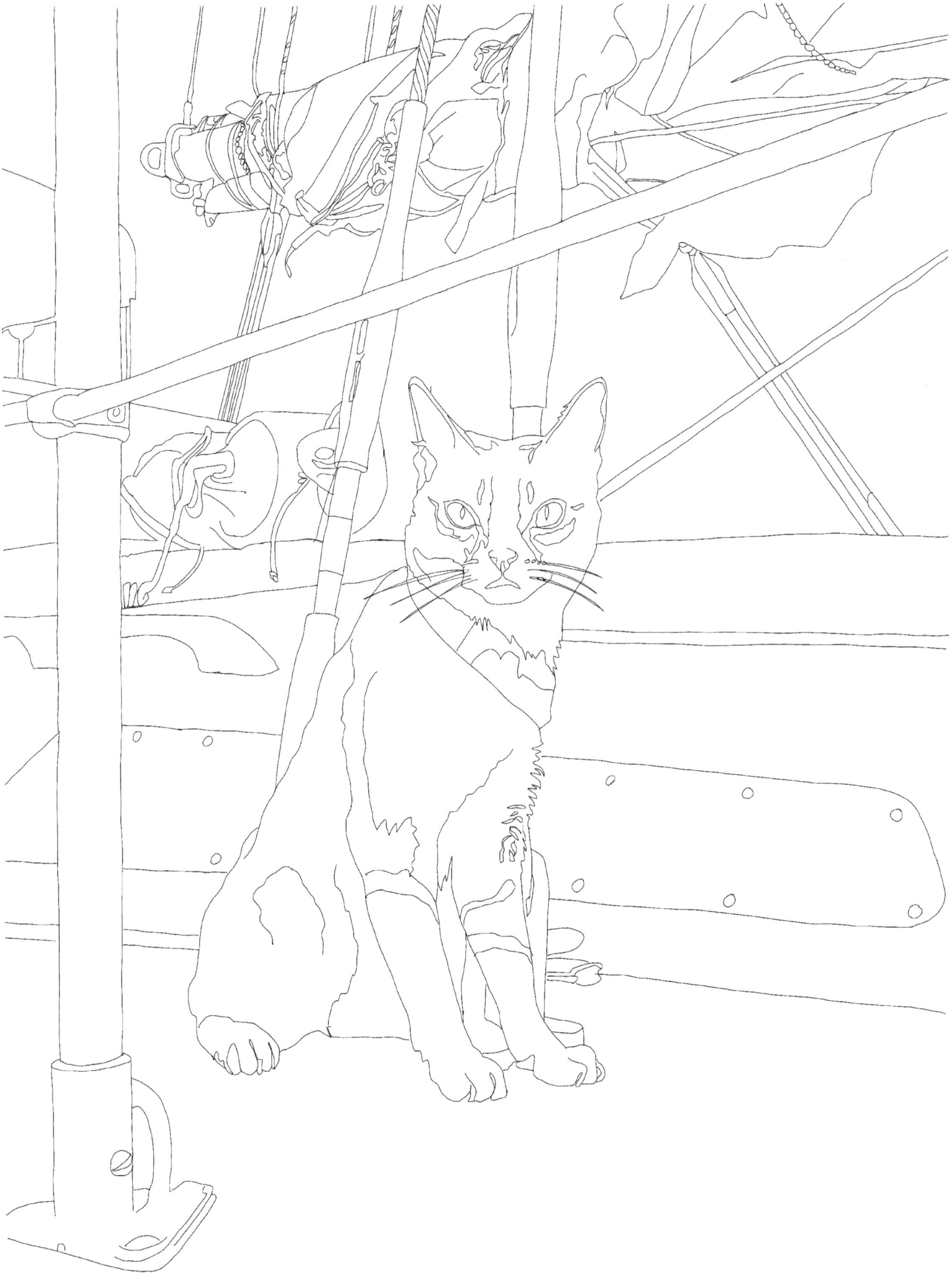

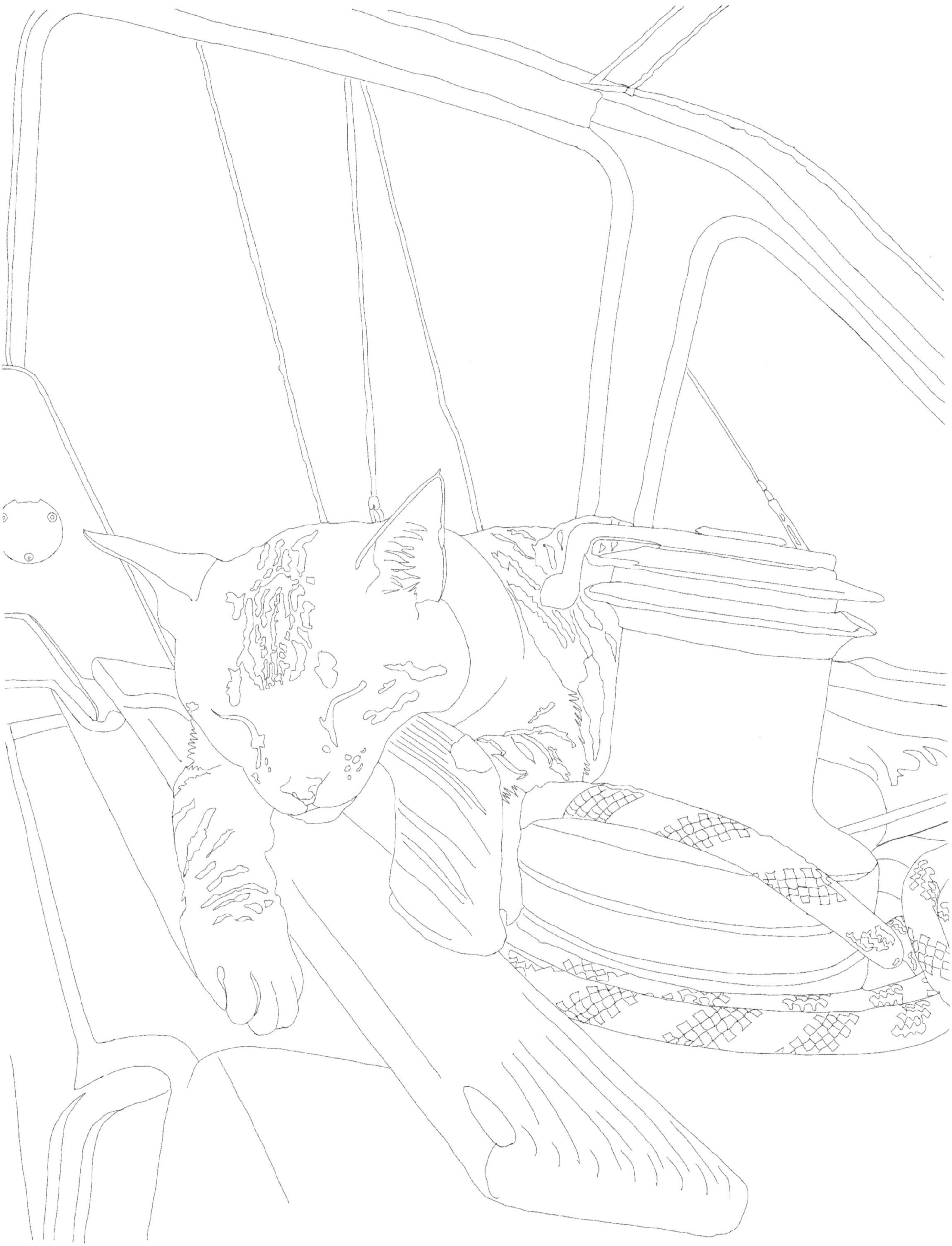

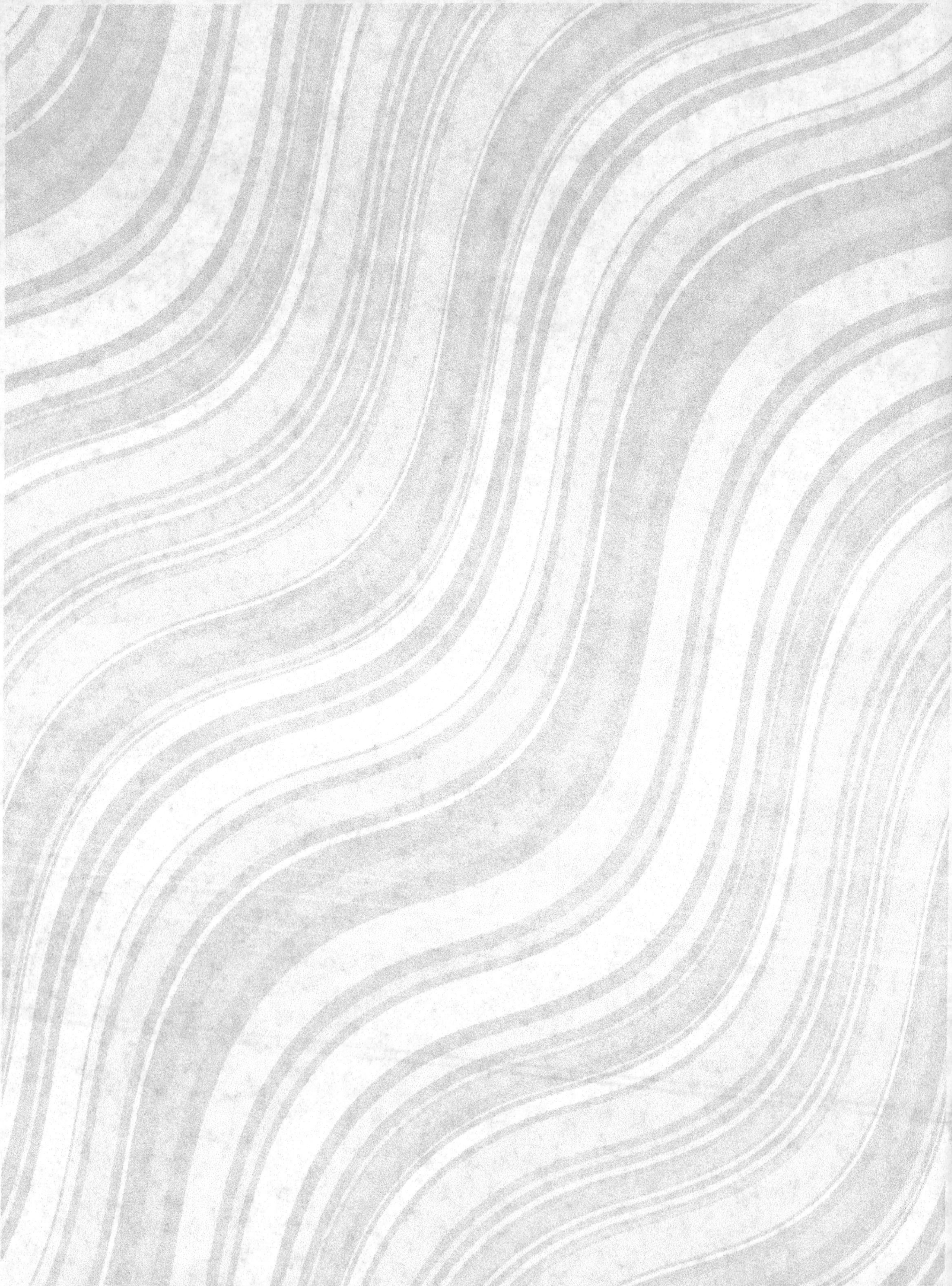

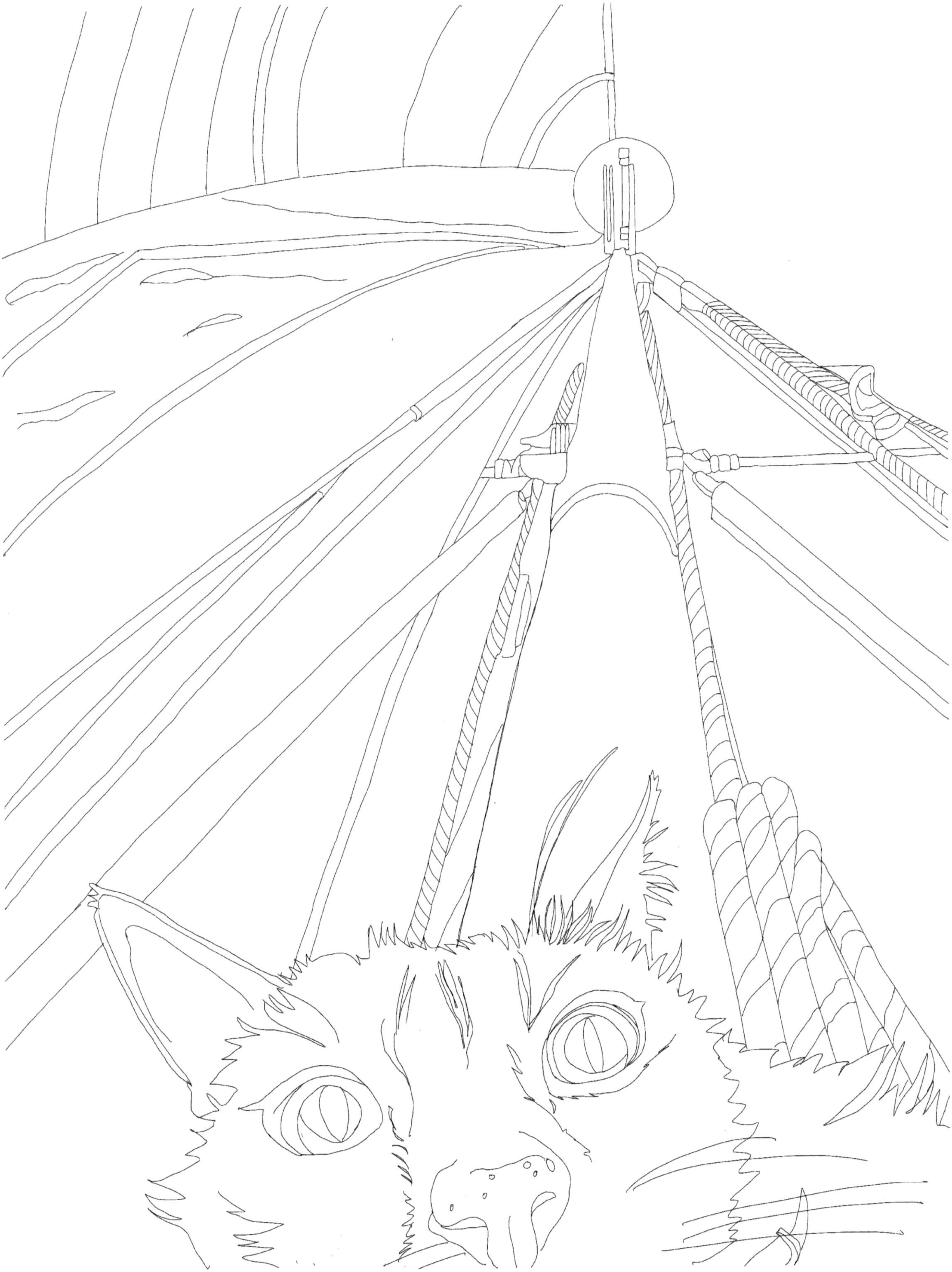

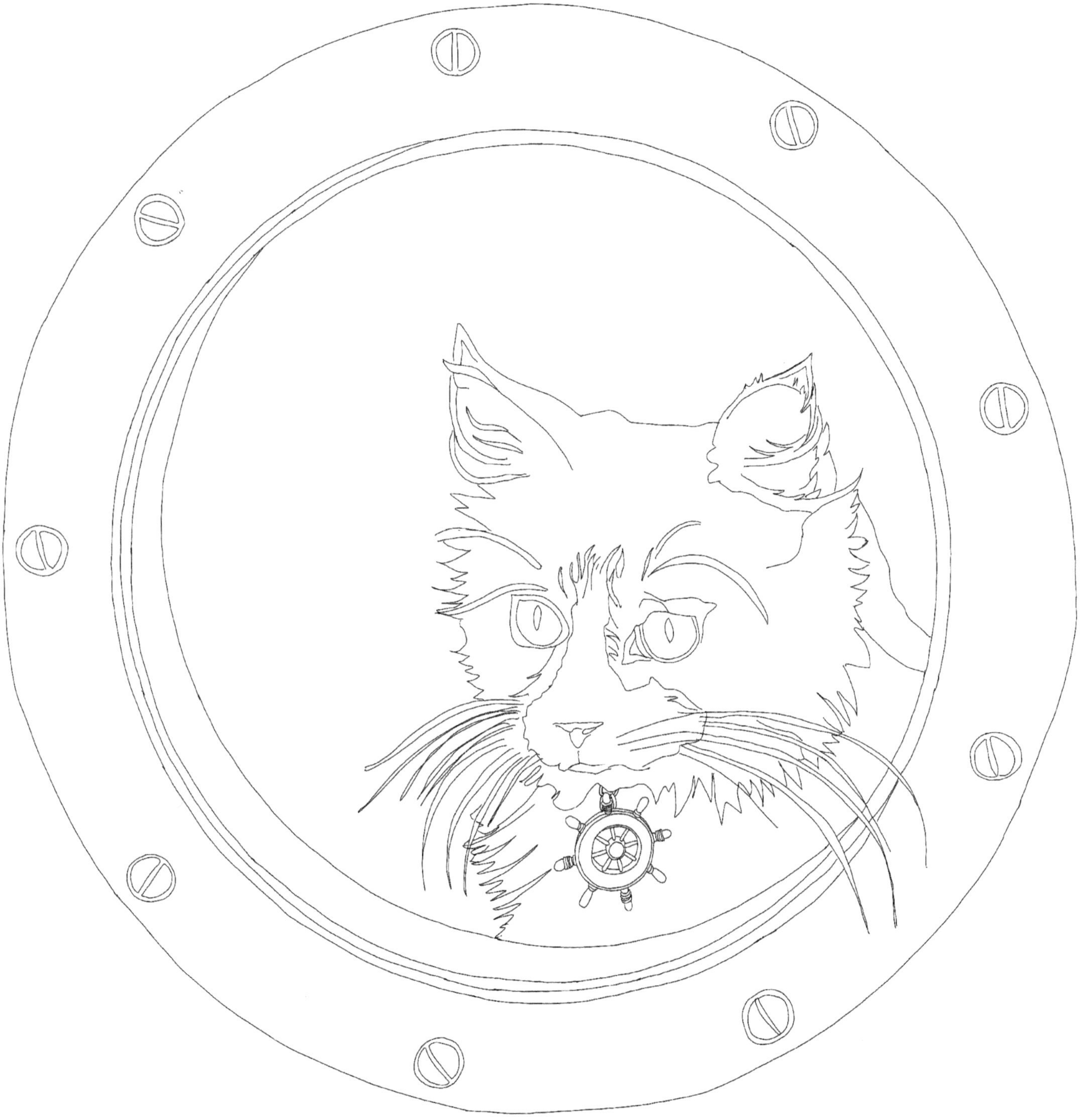

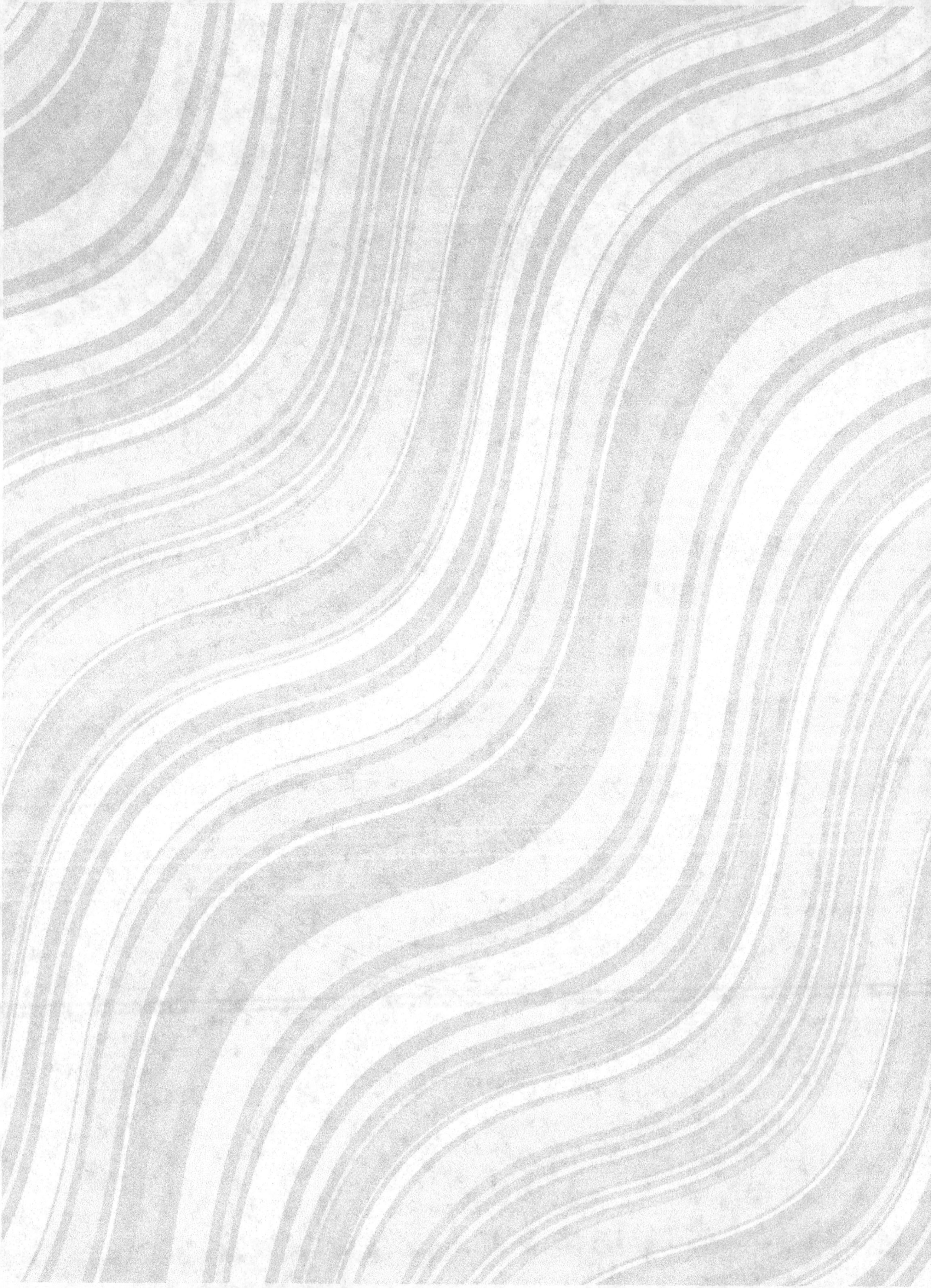

Find us at

@marinazaleart

www.ingramcontent.com/pod-product-compliance
Lightning Source LLC
Chambersburg PA
CBHW080559220526
45466CB00010B/3200
* 9 7 9 8 5 3 4 1 5 0 0 4 9 *